Anonymous

Scripture Record of the Life and Times of Samuel the Prophet

Anonymous

Scripture Record of the Life and Times of Samuel the Prophet

ISBN/EAN: 9783337053727

Printed in Europe, USA, Canada, Australia, Japan

Cover: Foto ©Lupo / pixelio.de

More available books at **www.hansebooks.com**

SCRIPTURE RECORD

OF THE

LIFE AND TIMES

OF

SAMUEL THE PROPHET.

BY THE AUTHOR OF
"SCRIPTURE RECORD OF THE BLESSED VIRGIN,
THE MOTHER OF OUR LORD."

"Seek ye out of the book of the Lord, and read: no one of these shall fail, none shall want her mate:"—ISA. xxxiv. 16.

London;
RIVINGTONS, 3, WATERLOO PLACE:
AND 41, HIGH STREET,
Oxford.
1863.

CONTENTS.

	PAGE
Introduction	v

CHAPTER I.
The Birth and Presentation of Samuel 1

CHAPTER II.
The Call of Samuel in the Temple 8

CHAPTER III.
Taking of the Ark by the Philistines 17

CHAPTER IV.
The Ark sent back to Kirjath-jearim 26

CHAPTER V.
Samuel made Judge over Israel 36

CHAPTER VI.
Samuel consecrates Saul first king in Israel . . . 44

CHAPTER VII.
Samuel takes leave of his people 56

CHAPTER VIII.

Saul reproved by Samuel for taking upon himself the Priest's office 66

CHAPTER IX.

Saul again reproved by Samuel, and finally rejected from being king over Israel 74

CHAPTER X.

Samuel commanded to consecrate David . . . 89

CHAPTER XI.

Samuel consecrates David at Bethlehem to be king instead of Saul 95

CHAPTER XII.

The Death of Samuel 105

CHAPTER XIII.

Saul seeks after a woman with a familiar spirit . . 113

CHAPTER XIV.

The raising of Samuel at Endor 122

CHAPTER XV.

Battle of Mount Gilboa 132

CHAPTER XVI.

Conclusion 144

INTRODUCTION.

IT has been truly and beautifully said by the late Archer Butler, in his admirable sermon on "Christ sought and found in the Old Testament Scriptures," that "*Expectation* is the inward spirit of the Old Testament, as *Fulfilment* of the New; wonderful itself, its function clearly is to testify wonders more august to come; . . . . . the Old Testament Scriptures overladen by one sect of Jews, curtailed by another, candidly studied by none, witnessed internally to a mighty future." "I pass not," he proceeds, "beyond its own pages, I ask not whence it came, nor how, I ask no external confirmations from contemporary history; I interrogate the Book alone, and its answer is unequivocal. Nay, in this view, its answer is often most direct when its language is most obscure. That mysterious volume, so large, so various, whose remotest authors are a thousand years asunder, had a single character, and that character was *pro-*

missory. *That* still follows it through all its many styles and all its mazy windings; *that* still is found —yea, more distinctly caught—in the dim recesses of those half-revealings, where it whispers more than it speaks aloud. It is, in truth, as some vast forest,—its own Lebanon or Carmel,—dusky and shadowy, yet with wondrous breaks and glimpses of sudden light, strange shapes and spectres in the gloom, and sometimes darkness thick as midnight: but a majestic spirit haunts the obscure immense,—the spirit of the future. Its presence startles us when we least expect it, and we walk with reverence and godly fear, feeling that all we see is holy, and all we see not is holier still."

This eloquent passage, though too long for a quotation, has nevertheless been given in full, for nowhere has the prophetical nature of the Old Testament Scriptures been more ably set forth, and to no portion of the Sacred Record do these beautiful words more strictly apply than to that portion of it chosen for our consideration in the following pages. For though the Book of Samuel was written upwards of a thousand years before the Christian era, its " promissory character " is clearly discerned in the typical events which it records: every where do these remarkable events speak to us of Him, who is the " object of the prophecies, the end of the miracles, and the *inner sense* of all the Jewish religion[1];" they speak to us of the sufferings of Christ, and of "the glory which should follow;" they speak to us of His first coming to be despised and rejected, "a man of sorrows and acquainted with grief;" they speak to us of His second coming "to be admired of all them that believe," and to reign over a people "made willing in the day of His power." At Shiloh, at Ramah, at Mizpeh, at Bethlehem, at Gilgal, at Gilboa, " that majestic spirit, the spirit of the future," startles us when we least expect it; for in the deeply interesting biographies of Samuel, of Saul, and of David, the Christian reader is enabled to recognize a grand historical prophecy, shadowing forth still greater things to come.

[1] See Alexandre Vinet on the writings of Pascal.

CHAPTER I.

THE BIRTH AND PRESENTATION OF SAMUEL.

HANNAH the wife of Elkanah had been for the first years of her married life a woman of a sorrowful spirit, for God had denied her the blessing so dearly coveted by Hebrew women. Year after year she had gone up childless to worship at the Temple of the Lord; and as on the solemn and joyous festivals of the Church she saw herself surrounded by the happy mothers of the sons and daughters of Israel, her deprivation was more acutely felt and more deeply deplored. On these trying occasions it was in vain that Elkanah endeavoured to cheer the drooping spirit of his much-loved and favourite wife. In vain did he bestow upon her the worthiest portion in token of his tender affection; she refused to be comforted, "she wept and would not eat." It was all in vain that he fondly remonstrated with her for giving way to this obstinate grief, saying "Hannah, why weepest thou? and why eatest thou not? and why is thy heart grieved? Am I not better to thee than ten sons?" Doubtless he was better, a thousand times better, to her than any other earthly blessing; but she knew that, though it found no utterance, the same ardent desire that agitated her bosom was secretly shared by her husband; for his sake, therefore, as well as for her own, she sought from the God of all consolation the removal of her grief, and so long and so perseveringly did she wait upon Him, that at length her prayer was heard, the desire of her heart was accomplished, and her hitherto desolate home was gladdened with the presence of a son.

There is joy in the lofty mansions of the great, when the long-desired heir is sent at last to crown their cup of earthly prosperity. There is joy, too, in the lowly dwellings of the poor, when the loving mother clasps her first-born to her bosom, and thinks herself rich in the smiles of her babe. But in the home of the Israelite, to the human feelings natural on such an occasion, there was added a deep, mysterious joy; for the promise first given in Paradise, that the seed of the woman should bruise the serpent's head, was treasured up in the heart of the pious like the manna in the golden vessel of the Sanctuary, and by appropriating this glorious promise to themselves on the advent of their first-born, the happy parents seemed to enjoy a foretaste of the exultation of the prophet, when in after times he triumphantly exclaimed, "Unto us a child is born: unto us a son is given!"

The wife of Elkanah, when she prayed for a son, had vowed that if her prayer were granted, she would devote that son to the Lord all the days of his life—"that he might appear before the Lord, and there abide for ever:" nor in the narrative before us is there the slightest indication of a faltering purpose, or even a desire to withdraw from the strict fulfilment of her vow. On the contrary, in the outward bearing of the childless wife of Elkanah and that of the happy mother of Samuel, there was a very remarkable contrast; for the vehement, and it might seem unreasonable, impatience which characterized the conduct of Hannah before the birth of her son was succeeded by the deep tranquillity, the perfect peace of one whose heart is at rest, and whose mind is stayed upon her God; nor was there any reason why it should be otherwise, for in dedicating her Samuel to the service of the Lord, Hannah knew that she was seeking the highest good for her child; she knew that she was leading him to the "upper springs" of heavenly joy and gladness, without shutting him out hereafter from those "nether springs" of domestic felicity which a God of mercy has graciously opened in the wilderness of this world, to refresh the weary pilgrim in his journey through life. There was no presumptuous attempt to sever those holy ties which God Himself has knit together, and which it is permitted to no man to put asunder; for in offering Samuel to the Lord the fond mother had but drawn together more closely the tie which bound her to her child; she was still his mother, he was still her son; she knew that every year as she went up to worship at the Temple, she might in unrestricted intercourse clasp her child in her arms, and clothe him in the garments woven by her loving hand, and watch him as he increased in wisdom and in stature, and, true type of his Redeemer, in favour with God and with man; and when he grew on to manhood she knew that she might bless the wife of his bosom, and the children which God might give him; and that as long as she lived, she might seek wisdom and comfort from his lips, that his much-loved hand might close her eyes in death, and his tender voice bid her spirit depart in peace. Thus was Hannah's dedication of her son to the service of the Lord not a superstitious offering, but a reasonable sacrifice, brought not "grudgingly nor of necessity," but with a cheerful and loving spirit, and with only that wise delay which nature demanded, and which she knew that her God would approve; for when Elkanah, after the birth of Samuel, goes up to worship and to offer the yearly sacrifice, she said to her husband, "I will not go up until the child be weaned, and then I will bring him, that he may appear before the Lord, and there abide for ever." And Elkanah her husband said unto her, "Do what seemeth thee good, tarry until thou have weaned him; only the Lord establish His word." Thus Hannah remained at home to tend and cherish her heart's best treasure, that she might present him at the appointed time to the gracious Being from whom she had received him.

> "So have I seen, in spring's bewitching hour,
> When the glad earth is offering all her best,
> Some gentle maid bend o'er a cherish'd flower
> And wish it worthier on a parent's heart to rest."

Accordingly, we read that when Hannah weaned her son, she brought him unto the house of the Lord in Shiloh; and as if to show that there had been no backwardness in the fulfilment of her vow, it is expressly added that "the child was young" when thus consecrated to the service of the Temple. At the moment of parting, if some natural tears fell from the mother's eye, they must have been but like the drops which escape from a passing cloud on a summer's day, glittering as they fall in the bright rays of the sunshine around them; for on bringing her gift to the altar, the happy mother of Samuel, like the blessed mother of the Saviour, breaks forth into a glorious hymn of praise and thanksgiving, in which she magnifies the Lord, and rejoices in the salvation of her God.

It is very remarkable that some of the most beautiful songs of praise in Holy Scripture are put into the mouth of the woman, as if she who had been first in the transgression was graciously privileged to be foremost in celebrating the removal of the curse. It was Miriam the prophetess, who led her people in the wilderness, to glorify God, saying, "Sing ye to the Lord; for He hath triumphed gloriously: the horse and the rider hath He thrown into the sea;" it was Deborah, a mother in Israel, who was called upon "to awake, and to utter a song," to celebrate the victory of the Lord over the mighty, when the stars fought against Sisera, when "captivity was led captive," when the strength of God was perfected in weakness, and the great adversary of His people was made to bow down at the feet of a woman; it was the wife of Elkanah, and the mother of the Saviour, who were privileged to sing of a more glorious triumph, to celebrate a mightier deliverance, not from the host of the Egyptian, or of the Assyrian, but from principalities and powers, and spiritual wickedness in high places; they sing not of the battle of the warrior, "which is with confused noise, and garments rolled in blood;" not the going forth of one mighty to destroy, but of one mighty to save; they sing by anticipation the triumph of the King of righteousness, and the victory of the Prince of peace. Both these sacred hymns proclaim almost in the self-same words the goodness of God in the land of the living, and His faithfulness in fulfilling the promises which He made to Abraham and his seed for ever.

But as a prophecy the song of Hannah is more comprehensive than that of the Virgin; for it seems to have been given to the mother of Samuel to embrace in her vision the beginning and the end of this earthly dispensation, to pierce through the shadows of time, and to gaze upon the glories of eternity. Forgetting her own individuality and the circumstances under which her thanksgiving was offered, looking beyond the type to the antitype, she speaks of the time when the barren will bear seven; "when more will be the children of the desolate than of her that hath an husband;" when God will give to His people "a name better than of sons and of daughters,"—an everlasting name, which shall not be cut off. She speaks, too, of Him, who is "the resurrection and the life;" who killeth and maketh alive; "who bringeth down to the grave, and bringeth up;" who "raiseth the poor out of the dust, and lifteth up the beggar from the dunghill" to set him among princes, and to make him "inherit the throne of glory;" she hears the voice of Him, who has said, "The earth is weak, and the inhabitants thereof: I bear up the pillars of it;" for she declares that the "pillars of the earth are the Lord's, and that He hath set the world upon them;" and, finally, she looks forward to that great day, when the adversaries of the Lord will be broken in pieces; when He will "thunder upon them out of Heaven;" when He will "judge the ends of the earth;" when He will "give strength to His King;" when He will exalt the horn of His Anointed.

CHAPTER II.

THE CALL OF SAMUEL IN THE TEMPLE.

It must have been a moment of deep interest to the High Priest of the Tabernacle when the mother of Samuel presented herself before him at Shiloh with the offering she had brought to the house of the Lord; for Hannah was no stranger to Eli. Before the birth of her son, while engaged in the Temple in earnest and fervent prayer, something remarkable about her had attracted the observation of the aged Priest; and we are told that while she continued praying, "he had marked her mouth;" for as her feelings were too deep to find utterance in words, "she spake in her heart, only her lips moved, but her voice was not heard;" and so, for a moment, Eli was tempted to class the pious wife of Elkanah with the daughters of Belial, who were wont, with their evil practices, to desecrate the courts of the house of the Lord. Hannah, wrongfully accused of intemperance, and angrily reproached for her shame, firmly, but with reverence and meekness, repels the unjust suspicion; she declares that she is a woman of a sorrowful spirit, that she had but "poured out her grief unto the Lord," and that "out of the abundance of her grief and complaint she had spoken hitherto." Moved by her touching reply, Eli atones at once for his rash condemnation by dismissing her with a blessing, and a prayer that the God of Israel would grant her the petition she had asked of Him. But now this same woman once more stands before him anxious, not to call to mind his former unjust and cruel accusation, but to tell him of the prayer she had offered, and to show him that God had most graciously answered that prayer. And when, after having thus recorded her past sorrow and her present joy, she piously consigns her Samuel to the future superintendence of the High Priest of the Tabernacle, a pang of self-reproach must surely have gone through the heart of the aged Eli, for he must at that moment have contrasted the true and disinterested love of Hannah for her child, in thus seeking for him "first the Kingdom of God and His righteousness," with the foolish fondness *he* had shown towards his own unhappy offspring: bitterly must he have lamented that a long course of misplaced and highly culpable indulgence had struck at the root of parental authority, and made him the victim instead of the guide of his children; leaving him to grieve over the wickedness which he had now no power to restrain.

The son of Hannah, however, was intended by God to do something more than by his presence to remind the erring parent of the sins of the past.

Immediately upon his presentation at the Temple,

the boy, clad in a linen ephod, "ministered unto the Lord" before Eli, performing those light and easy duties which were fitted to his tender years, and, doubtless, looking forward with childish delight to the happy time when his fond mother would come again to Shiloh, and array him in the little garment, worked by her loving hands.

This blessed tranquillity was not, however, to remain long undisturbed; Samuel, young as he was, must soon be taught to suffer, and to obey. For not merely was he to be one of God's most distinguished Prophets, but he was also to be the *only* one called, while yet a child, to exercise his sacred office, and to hear the voice of the Lord, even before he had been taught how he was to answer it.

From the days of Joshua to the judgeship of Eli, no great Prophet had been given to Israel, and God had ceased to manifest His presence to His people in the visible brightness and glory of the Shekinah. We are therefore told, that "the word of the Lord was precious in those days," and that "there was no open vision;" and the sacred writer, after having thus intimated the spiritual destitution of Israel at that period of our history, goes on to describe a scene which has no parallel in Holy Writ; for as in the phenomena of the natural world, the lightning that destroys has been seen to flash in awful contrast from a sky on whose pure surface no cloud was to be seen, so it pleased the Almighty once, and only once, to make the young and innocent child a messenger of His wrathful indignation to the aged and sinful man.

The day with its appointed work was over in the Temple at Shiloh. The solemn services of the Sanctuary were at an end. The sacrifices of the Law had been offered up, and the cry of God's innocent creation, groaning and travailing in pain for the transgression of His people, no longer resounded through the court of the Tabernacle. The voice of prayer, and praise, and thanksgiving had also died away; for God has given "unto life's fainting traveller the night" to rest from the toil of the day, and to seek strength for the journey of the morrow.

In spite of the corruption of the priesthood during the judgeship of Eli, the sacred ordinances of the Temple had not been neglected; the holy fire, which, like the vital spark in the soul of man, had been first kindled from above, was still kept alive on the altar of burnt sacrifice, and the lights of the Sanctuary were still kept burning before Him, "who sat between the cherubims;" for we are told that it was "ere the lamp of God went out" in the Temple of the Lord, "where the Ark of God was," that Samuel, fatigued with the pleasant duties of his office, had laid him down to sleep. The High Priest Eli was also "laid down in his place" to seek that rest for the wearied body, which he could not find for the wounded spirit. He was blind from age, perhaps from weeping; and many must have been the painful thoughts which kept sleep from those poor dim eyes!

What a picture of life at its beginning and life at its close is presented to our contemplation, as we gaze upon the youthful boy, and the aged man!—the one sunk in the peaceful slumbers of childhood's happy dreams which, like stars, make the night for him as bright as the day; and the other, to whom the night brings no repose, for the remembrance of the past agitates his bosom;—his children's ingratitude, "sharper than a serpent's tooth," goes through his soul, and, worse than all, a "certain fearful looking for of judgment and fiery indignation to come," presses sorely on a conscience ill at ease with itself!

An awful silence reigned in the Temple of the Lord, broken only by the gentle breathings of the sleeping boy, and the heavy sighs of the aged Priest. They seemed to be alone; they were, however, not alone; for Thou wast there,—Thou

> "Who didst wrap the cloud
> Of infancy around us, that Thyself
> Therein with our simplicity awhile
> Might hold on earth communion undisturbed."

Thou wast there, and about to reveal Thy sacred presence to the outward senses of the young child; not by the fire, the earthquake, or the whirlwind, but by a still small voice, which gently arouses the boy from his slumbers. The voice which called

Samuel by name was like that of Eli. It may be that the Father of all mercies thus assumed the familiar sound of the beloved instructor's voice, in order that He might not frighten the sleeping boy, and perhaps also to show that when He speaks to the heart of the young, it is through the instrumentality of the parent, or the spiritual instructor. Twice did Samuel hear the call repeated, and twice did he hasten to the couch of Eli, who each time dismissed him with the injunction to lie down again, and the assurance that he called him not. When however the voice came a third time, Eli immediately recognized the interposition of the Triune Jehovah, the "Holy, holy, holy Lord God of Hosts," and bids the boy return once more to his bed, and should the call be repeated, immediately to answer, "Speak, Lord; for Thy servant heareth."

Let us pause for a moment, and remark how faithful God ever is to His own ordinances; how rarely His mighty power interferes with the moral and providential laws given as guides to His children here below; for though He needed not the intervention of His minister, as He could in an instant have revealed His own will to His youthful servant, still He withholds the revelation of that will until the boy has been prepared to receive it; for as yet we are told, "Samuel knew not the Lord," that is, he had not yet been instructed in the reverential form of words by which the Deity was to be addressed, and the divine communications received. He must, therefore, learn from the lips of his spiritual teacher, from the erring minister of the Temple, how he is to answer, should the Lord again vouchsafe to call him by his name. In childlike submission Samuel receives the instructions of Eli; he returns to his bed, lays himself down, and silently awaits the coming again of that mysterious voice, which had thrice aroused him from his sleep. He does not wait in vain. It comes again; and this time not only is a voice heard, but a presence is indicated; for it is now particularly said, "the Lord came, and stood, and called as before, Samuel, Samuel." The boy, true to the instructions he had received, reverently answers, "Speak; for Thy servant heareth." God's sentence is then irrevocably pronounced against the house of Eli,—a sentence involving the sorest punishment which could be inflicted upon an Israelite,—the rejection of his posterity, and their exclusion for ever from the honourable distinction of the priesthood.

After uttering this condemnation, the mysterious voice is heard no more. The Divine Presence is withdrawn, and the child Samuel is left alone to think over the words he has heard, and to keep them in his heart.

When, on Mount Horeb, the Almighty spoke to Moses, the lawgiver trembled and "durst not behold." When the assembled multitudes of Israel heard the awful voice of God, they prayed that they might never be constrained to listen to it again. When Eliphaz, in the visions of the night, heard a voice saying, "Can a mortal man be more just than his Maker?" "the hair on his head stood up." When Elijah heard the "still small voice" of God, full of awful dread, he shrouded his face in his mantle. When God revealed Himself to Isaiah, the prophet cried out, "Woe is me, for I am a man of unclean lips;" and when to Daniel, even the man greatly beloved "fell down as one dead at His feet." But in this manifestation of the Divine Presence to the child Samuel, all is calm, all is peaceful; the only fear that oppresses that youthful spirit is the fear of telling Eli the vision, the fear of carrying grief and dismay into the bosom of his kind and beloved preceptor. The boy, after receiving his high commission, laid him down till the morning, watching, we may believe, anxiously and sorrowfully for the dawn of the coming day. It comes at last, and Samuel with heavy heart must rise to open the doors of the Temple; but still he withholds the terrible message, for he "fears to tell Eli the vision." Sad forebodings of evil arise in the mind of the minister of the Sanctuary, confirmed doubtless by no longer hearing the merry sound of the child's early carol; something too in the boy's very footstep might tell of the weight which was bearing down that young and joyous spirit; but as Samuel will not, cannot bring himself to break this terrible silence, the old man can bear the misery of suspense no longer: he feels that it is better to know the worst at once, and summoning up resolution to meet the blow, he thus emphatically adjures the boy to hide nothing from him:

"Then Eli called Samuel, and said, Samuel, my son. And he answered, Here am I. And he said, What is the thing that the Lord hath said unto thee? I pray thee hide it not from me: God do so to thee, and more also, if thou hide any thing from me of all the things that He said unto thee [1]."

Thus solemnly adjured, Samuel tells him every whit; he presumes not to add nor to take away one word from the message which he had been charged to deliver.

Thus the weight falls from the mind of the young child, but it does not crush the aged man; for, as the ancient tree of the forest, which the lightning has scathed, and the whirlwind has shorn of its leaves and fruit, may still be seen to hold its ground, stretching forth its naked branches, in attitude of supplication to the power that has blasted it—so stands the aged servant of the Lord, his withered arms upraised to Heaven, humbly embracing the will of God, as if it were his own will, and meekly, and devoutly exclaiming, "It is the Lord: let Him do what seemeth Him good."

[1] 1 Sam. iii.

CHAPTER III.

TAKING OF THE ARK BY THE PHILISTINES.

AFTER God's wonderful manifestation of His divine presence in the Temple, we find but little recorded of the youth of Samuel, except that, like his divine antitype, he grew and was in favour not only with the Lord, but also with man, and that his words were none of them suffered to fall to the ground, but were all made to accomplish the purpose for which they were spoken. Yet, like the words spoken by the child Jesus, which, for their wisdom, astonished, and for three days held captive the doctors of the law in the Temple of Jerusalem, not one of the words of the youthful Samuel has been recorded by the sacred penman, so contrary does it seem to the will of God that the sayings of the young should ever be cited, or they themselves brought forward except as examples of humility and obedience; for these are the graces of youth, and these were the graces which peculiarly distinguished the early years of Samuel as well as the early years of the Holy One of Israel of whom he was so remarkable a type.

Greatly must it have cheered the heart of the aged Eli to watch the growth of this beautiful shoot of the Lord's planting, "flourishing in the courts of the house of our God," and bringing forth such lovely fruits of righteousness, that "all Israel, from Dan to Beersheba, knew that Samuel was established to be a prophet of the Lord." Eli, though totally unfit to curb the turbulent and reckless spirit of his own children, was nevertheless well qualified to tend and develope the humble and pious disposition of the son of Hannah. Devoted to the care of his youthful charge, the old man's withered heart must have recovered its freshness; he must have felt that God, in giving him Samuel, had not "shut up His loving-kindness in displeasure." Perhaps, as the terrible judgments pronounced against his house had been delayed, he might have indulged a hope that they would never be executed; for the sin of Eli seems to have been too exclusive and entire a dependence upon God's mercy, without a due apprehension of His truth and of His justice. God's mercy, however, being without partiality, cannot show itself only to the sinner; it must also extend itself to those who are sinned against; so that if the offending member, though long borne with, cannot be healed, it must, for the preservation of the body, be cut off at last. Thus it was with the unhappy sons of Eli: they had persevered so daringly and so wilfully in their sinful practices, that grace long resisted was at length withdrawn; and as by their life they had taught men to break the commandments of the Lord, so by their death they must teach men to fear His awful judgments, and to believe that as truly as there is a reward for the righteous, so truly there is a God that judgeth the earth. The fierce and constant foes of Israel are now to be made the instrument in the hand of God to punish both the priest and the people for desecrating His Temple and forsaking His commandments; and those who had so often experienced His power to save, must now be made to feel His power to destroy.

The Philistines, we read, "put themselves in array against Israel, and when they joined battle, Israel was smitten before the Philistines, and they slew of the army in the field four thousand men." And when the people were come into the camp, the elders of Israel said, "Wherefore hath the Lord smitten us to-day before the Philistines?" The presumptuous question was asked in a spirit of rage and disappointment; nor was there found any true and honest enough to answer, "Because we have sinned against the Lord, and provoked most justly His wrath and indignation against us." Instead of humbling themselves before that Great Power who they acknowledged was smiting them, the arrogance of their language in thus questioning the Almighty was followed by the still greater presumption of attempting to coerce His Almighty power by unlawfully seizing the sacred Ark of the Covenant, and bringing it into the camp. For the elders of Israel said, "Let us fetch the Ark of the Covenant of the Lord out of Shiloh unto us, that when it cometh among us, it may save us out of the hand of our enemies." So the people sent to Shiloh, that they might bring from thence the Ark of the Covenant of the Lord of Hosts, which dwelleth between the cherubims: and the two sons of Eli, Hophni and Phinehas, were there, with the Ark of the Covenant of God.

The elders said, " Bring the Ark forth that *it* may save us;" and the two sons of Eli, those desperately wicked men, instead of resisting this profane expedient, listened to the voice of the people, and sacrilegiously bore the sacred symbol of God's presence into the camp of Israel. "And when the Ark of the Covenant of the Lord came into the camp, all Israel shouted with a great shout, so that all the earth rang again."

Terrible was the consternation of the Philistines when they heard that enthusiastic shout. "Woe unto us," they cried, "woe unto us, for God is come into the camp." Still the courage of those poor heathens did not forsake them; for their next cry was, "Be strong, and quit yourselves like men," and they did quit themselves like men, for they fought desperately and conquered; and the Ark of God was taken, not, however, before the two sons of Eli had fallen bravely in its defence. While alive, these wretched sinners had violated the commandments of the God of the Tabernacle, and profaned its sanctity with their iniquities; and yet these very men were found ready to lay down their lives to preserve the outward sign of God's holy presence from falling into the hand of the enemy.

Thus has it often been with the symbol of our most holy faith: men bearing in their hands the cross of the Redeemer, without any true faith in Him who hung upon it,—men clinging to the outward sign, without a thought of Him who gave to that sign its power and its sanctity,—men of fanatical passions and vicious lives,—have made an idol of that "blessed wood whereby righteousness cometh[1];" have profanely said with the elders of Israel, "It shall save us;" have carried it into the battle-field; have fought desperately; and like the sons of Eli, have fallen bravely in defence of what to them was but a vain and empty shadow, instead of a substantial and living reality; so true is it that to die for the religion we profess is easier far than to live in conformity to its holy and blessed precepts.

The Gentiles having thus violently wrested from Israel the sacred Ark of the first covenant, all is now dismay in the camp of the Israelites; the shout of enthusiasm which had made the earth ring again is succeeded by a cry of despair, a cry which reached even to Shiloh, where the unfortunate Eli, in an agony of suspense, was waiting anxiously to receive

[1] See Wisdom xiv. 7.

the first tidings from the camp; for "his heart trembled for the Ark of the Lord," and when Eli heard the noise of the crying, he said, "What meaneth the noise of this tumult?" and a man came in hastily and told Eli. "Now Eli was ninety and eight years old, and his eyes were dim that he could not see." "And the man said unto Eli, I am he that came out of the army, and I fled to-day out of the camp." And Eli said, "What is there done, my son?" Thus questioned, the messenger tells him that Israel had fled before the victorious Philistines, and that Hophni and Phinehas had both fallen on the field of battle. It must indeed have been a sore trial for the miserable parent to hear that in one day he had been thus left childless; but knowing that the punishment, though severe, was just, his meek spirit might again have bowed in pious resignation to the will of the Almighty. Heavier tidings, however, remained behind; tidings of such bitterness, that upon hearing them, the aged servant of the Lord fell a lifeless corpse from the throne on which he had so long, and alas! so feebly judged his people. That the glory had departed from Israel, that the Ark of God was taken, were not only to the minister of the Temple tidings of despair and death, but so were they also to the young mother, the wife of Phinehas, who having just given birth to a son, sank under the weight of this terrible national calamity. In vain did the women who tended her attempt to revive her drooping spirit by the joyful news that a man was born into the world; it brought no joy now to the heart of the Hebrew mother; she never looked at her new-born son, she took him not to her bosom; her death-knell had sounded, the glory had departed from Israel, for the Ark of God was taken.

Deeply seated in the heart of the Israelites were the enthusiastic feelings with which they regarded the sacred Ark of the Tabernacle. It was to them, in a degree, what the incarnation of the Son of God is to us. By it they realized God's presence upon earth. By it the Gospel "was preached unto them*." In it was the mercy-seat, speaking to them of the forgiveness of sins, by the blood of the atonement. In it was the unchangeable manna, teaching them to look for the true bread from Heaven in a vessel pure as the gold seven times refined in the fire. In it was the rod of Aaron, life springing out of death, to teach them the doctrine of the resurrection. In it were the two tables of the covenant: the first by its spiritual application to the inner man, teaching them that without love to their Maker, faith in His Omnipresence, reverence for His worship, and obedience to those He had put in authority over them, it was impossible for them to please God; and the second, by its legal enactments and moral precepts, teaching them, that without practical holiness, no man could see the Lord.

* "To us was the Gospel preached as well as unto them," says St. Paul, speaking of the Israelites of old. Heb. iv. 2.

Their beloved Ark had ever been to them the pledge of God's favour; to it they looked for victory in warfare, assistance in trouble, security in danger; and now that it has fallen into the hands of the enemy, they seem to be abandoned for ever, and left without God in the world. No wonder, then, that a cry like that of Egypt, when death struck the firstborn in all their dwellings, rose up from the whole city; no wonder that the dying words of the wife of Phinehas found an echo in the heart of every bereaved Israelite. When, in after years, the Lord Jesus Christ was rudely seized by the heathen soldiery of Rome, just as the Ark was now seized by the heathen soldiery of the Philistine,—what, at that sad moment, became of the multitudes He had healed? of the thousands He had fed? and the tens of thousands He had comforted? There were no faithful Israelites then to make the bitter cry again resound through their city, "The glory is departed from Israel, for the Ark of God is taken!" A cry indeed was heard, so loud, so fearful, that at that awful sound, the sun hid its face, the earth shook, and the graves were opened; but it came from the cross of the Sufferer, not from the sorrowing hearts of His people Israel. For though once they had most truly believed that the Deity had graciously concentrated His glorious presence and dwelt amongst them, enshrined in the Ark of the Covenant, they afterwards refused to believe that the fulness of the Godhead had entered within a veil of flesh to tabernacle still more graciously amongst them, in the humanity of Jesus of Nazareth; and so a people who had once tenaciously clung to the type, gave up the antitype without a pang; for their deluded hearts knew not that it was then, and not till then, that the glory had indeed departed from Israel; that the true Ark of God was taken, that the angel of His presence had abandoned them, and that their house would henceforth be left unto them desolate, "until the times of the Gentiles should be fulfilled."

CHAPTER IV.

THE ARK SENT BACK TO KIRJATH-JEARIM.

THE success of the Philistines had been complete; the people of God had been entirely defeated, and their presumption deservedly punished by the capture of the Ark of the Covenant. But, though the loss of the Ark brought despair to the Israelites, its possession brought scarcely less consternation to their enemies; for wherever the Ark went, there went a miraculous and destructive influence along with it; and in order to propitiate this mighty power, the first thought which suggested itself to the darkened mind of the heathen was to take the Ark of the Lord to the temple of their god Dagon, and to set it up by the side of their idol divinity. In so doing these poor idolaters were sinning ignorantly, and a miraculous power was graciously put forth to instruct them if haply they might be brought to forsake the superstitious vanities of idolatry, and to cleave to the one only God. For this purpose life seems to be breathed for a moment into the senseless image of Dagon; it is made to tremble on its throne, and to fall prostrate before the sacred symbol of the presence of the Lord; for we read that "when the Philistines took the Ark of God, they brought it into the house of Dagon, and set it by Dagon." "And when they of Ashdod arose early on the morrow, behold, Dagon was fallen upon his face to the earth before the Ark of the Lord. And they took Dagon, and set him in his place again." Thus, uninfluenced even by this remarkable evidence of the power of God, with marvellous courage and fidelity to their fallen divinity, the men of Ashdod reverently raised him from the ground, and once more placed him by the side of the sacred Ark of the Covenant. Trembling for the safety of their God, these poor infatuated sinners again return at the dawn of day to the temple of Dagon, and find him not only prostrate a second time, but altogether annihilated. "The head of Dagon and both the palms of his hands were cut off upon the threshold; only the stump of Dagon was left to him:" type of the future destruction of all idolatry, head and hands, *thought* and *deed*. "For the day of the Lord shall be upon every one that is proud and lofty, and on every one that is lifted up, and upon all pleasant pictures. And the idols He shall utterly abolish, and they shall go into the holes of the rocks, and into the caves of the earth, for fear of the Lord, and for the glory of His Majesty, when He ariseth to shake terribly the earth." Very awful is it to behold in the history before us the power of superstition over the mind of man. The stones may cry out, but these Philistines remain unmoved. They see their God a mutilated trunk, but they will not bend the knee to the great Being who had thus so wonderfully instructed them; *they* will not fall prostrate by the side of their idol, and worship that Mighty Power which they feel, and which they acknowledge to be present amongst them. They *believe*, it is true, but like the devils they believe only to tremble; they believe, and are ready to show their faith by propitiatory offerings of jewels and gold; they are ready even to give glory to the God of Israel. In short, they are ready to sacrifice to Him any thing but their sins, to give Him any thing but their hearts. A *holy* God is a God they *will* not serve: had Dagon been holy they would not have worshipped him, for heathens as they are, they still feel and know that without any desire or intention to amend their ways and purify their hearts, prayer to a holy God would be an insult, worship a mockery. Terrified at His sanctity, their only desire is to get rid of so awful a presence out of their coasts. The priests of Dagon are consulted, and by their advice the Ark is sent with propitiatory offerings, and is brought into the field of Joshua, the Bethshemite, where it was welcomed with joy by the people, and where the Levites assembled to offer burnt sacrifice in honour of its restoration. This reverential feeling, however, was but of short continuance; the sacred Ark of the Covenant had been daringly removed from the Holy of Holies; it was no longer on consecrated ground;

it was no longer enclosed within the beautiful veil of the Tabernacle; it was no longer surrounded by faithful ministers appointed by God to guard its sanctity from the presumptuous scrutiny of the ignorant, and the irreverent handling of the profane. Divested of all its outward safeguards, the people vainly imagined they might draw near with unprepared hearts and unhallowed footsteps, rend aside the covering thrown over it whenever it was moved from the Holy of Holies, and curiously pry into what God had forbidden them to look into. Some bold and daring spirit, some Korah, Dathan, or Abiram, was doubtless there, to encourage and lead on the people to their destruction: perhaps by persuading them that all the congregation was equally holy, that Moses in giving the Law had spoken his own mind, and not the mind of God, and that the prohibition which made it death for any but the Levite to touch the sacred Ark of the Covenant, was the prohibition of man, not the prohibition of God. Whether seduced by the sophistry of others or led astray by their own folly and wilfulness and disobedience, these unhappy Bethshemites soon found out to their cost, that as the truth of God's word did not rest upon the faith of man, so neither could it be shaken by man's infidelity.

In our day we irreverently approach the Holy of Holies, and tread under foot all the sacred memories and associations of the past, and yet no angel is commissioned by God to slay us with " the blasting of the breath of His displeasure." We sharpen our wits, and make shreds of the book of the Law, and fondly imagine by some device of our own to steady and support what in ignorance we deem to be the falling Ark of the Lord; and yet no Almighty arm is stretched forth to punish on the spot our folly and presumption. Seeing as we do only in part, and knowing absolutely nothing as we ought to know it, we curiously pry into God's work, till we end by denying His Word,—

> "Though sweet the lore that nature brings,
>   Our meddling intellect
> Mis-shapes the beauteous form of things,—
>   We murder to dissect,"—

and yet no voice out of the whirlwind miraculously compels us to lay our "hand upon our mouth," and to confess that we uttered what we "understood not," and "darkened counsel by words without knowledge."

God does no "new thing[1]" in our day to

> "Shame the doctrine of the Sadducee,
> Or Sophist vainly mad of human lore."

In the days of old punishment quickly followed the offence. In the history before us the priests were slain for carrying the sacred Ark into the arena of strife and contention, and the people were slain for imitating the rashness and impiety of those appointed to instruct and to guide them.

[1] Numb. xvi. 30.

The sudden and terrible judgment which overtook the chief offenders in Bethshemesh, effectually awed the rest of the people into submission. Their daring infidelity was succeeded by abject superstition. They thought that by getting rid of the presence of the sacred Ark of the Covenant, they should also get rid of the presence of the God whose majesty they had so recklessly offended. In fear and trembling they cry out [2], "Who is able to stand before this holy Lord God? And they sent messengers to the inhabitants of Kirjath-jearim, saying, The Philistines have brought again the Ark of the Lord; come ye down, and fetch it up to you. And the men of Kirjath-jearim came, and fetched up the Ark of the Lord, and brought it into the house of Abinadab in the hill, and sanctified Eleazar his son to keep the Ark of the Lord." As the sacred Ark had been in the keeping of the tribe of Benjamin nearly 350 years, an important and significant change had thus taken place in the Divine economy; for God had taken "sore displeasure at Israel, so that He forsook the tabernacle in Shiloh, even the tent that He had pitched among them. Moreover, He refused the tabernacle of Joseph and chose the tribe of Judah and Mount Sion which He loved, and He built His sanctuary on high like the earth which He hath established for ever." From the time that the people of God presumptuously carried the Ark from Shiloh into the camp of Israel,

[2] 1 Sam. vi. 20 to end of ch. vii. 1.

saying (though God was smiting them) it should save them, the excellent glory which it had in the wilderness was withdrawn; and though that glory seemed partially to return in the days of Solomon, it was only for a time, as the Ark itself was altogether wanting in the second Temple built by Ezra, after the return of the Jews from the Babylonian captivity[s]. What finally became of this most sacred relic of the old dispensation is to this day involved in mystery. Some think it has been lost in the depths of the sea, others that it has been buried in the Holy Land, and that it will be once more restored. In the vision of the Apocalypse, the Temple of God was opened in heaven, and "then was seen in His Temple the Ark of the Covenant;" a plain indication to us where we are to look for the Ark of our salvation. To expect a restoration of the Ark of the first covenant would be contrary to the word of prophecy; for God, speaking by the mouth of His prophet Jeremiah, declares to His people that when He finally brings them to Zion and gives them pastors according to His own heart, "to feed them with knowledge and understanding;"

[s] It is recorded that the Roman soldiery, at the taking of Jerusalem, rushed with eager curiosity towards the Holy of Holies, expecting to see within the veil a representation of the Deity worshipped by the Jew: their surprise and disappointment was unbounded, when they found nothing but an awful void, which their darkened minds were unable to fill up with the unseen presence of the true and only God.

that when Jerusalem is called "the throne of the Lord, and all nations gathered into it, to the name of the Lord, to Jerusalem;" "in those days, saith the Lord, they shall say no more, The Ark of the Covenant of the Lord: neither shall it come to mind: neither shall they remember it; neither shall they visit it; neither shall that be done any more [4]." It would be contrary also to the providential care of the Almighty to expect a restoration of the Ark of shittim-wood, for He has in every age of the world in a very remarkable manner removed whatever might have proved, or had proved, a stumbling-block in the way of His people. The ark of Noah was never heard of when wanted no longer. The miraculous rod of Moses was never preserved. The rod of Aaron, and the golden pot with the manna, disappeared after the Ark had been profaned by the sin of the people. The brazen serpent, the very same that Moses lifted up in the wilderness, when gazed upon by those who forgot that they had been saved, not by the thing which they saw but by the Saviour of all [5], was given up by the pious in Israel to be plucked as a superstitious vanity from the sight of the eyes, and from the idolatrous adoration of the people [6].

[4] See Jer. iii.   [5] Wisd. xvi. 17.
[6] In like manner our Reformers surrendered the outward sign of their most holy faith, which they had looked upon with reverential piety and devoted love, and were content to hide the cross in their hearts, to imprint it invisibly on the

The Ark of the Covenant, though so carefully guarded and so costly and precious, entirely disappeared from the face of the earth, and what God had done to the Tabernacle at Shiloh, that did He to the Temple built by Solomon, when the people began to trust in the Temple, more than in the God who sanctified the Temple. "Therefore will I do unto this house which is called by My name *wherein ye trust*, and unto the place which I gave to you and to your fathers, as I have done to Shiloh." The Temple of Herod, when made a house of merchandise, and a den of thieves, was utterly destroyed; not one stone was left upon another; all its precious vessels were removed, so that absolutely nothing whatever remained of the beautiful and costly relics of the old dispensation. And may we not say the same of the new dispensation? Are not the apostolic writings silent with respect to the sacred relics of the new covenant? The cross on which the Saviour hung, the crown of thorns, the earth's great curse which encircled His sacred head, the nails which fastened Him, the shroud which enveloped Him, the napkin which bound His brow in death, the seamless vesture, and the divided garments, all were suffered to disappear, for no evidence whatever is given in Holy Writ that any of these

infant brow, in order that by thus committing it to the safe keeping of the Spirit, and thus covering it with the sacred wing of the dove, it might be rescued from the ignorant handling, and superstitious adoration of man.

sacred relics were ever preserved by the followers of our Lord. Nay, even the very sepulchre that once received His sacred body, is to this day a matter of uncertainty [7]; many legitimately disbelieve that the spot hallowed for centuries by the prayers and tears of the faithful, and desecrated by bloodshed, violence, fraud, and impiety, is really the place where He was laid. At any rate, of this we are certain, that though the tombs of the holy men of old do indeed contain the blessed seed of immortality, the body which, sown in "weakness, will be raised in power," it is not so with the sepulchre of Jesus. His "tomb is empty," for the earth could hold nothing of Him, and those who seek the living among the dead, seek for Him in vain. "He is not here, he is risen,"—risen "far above." all principality, and power, and might, and dominion, and every name that is named, not only in this world, but also in that which is to come [8]; for it was expedient that He too, in His human nature, should be removed from the sight of His people, in order that knowing Him no longer "after the flesh," they should henceforth see Him by the eye of faith, and learn to worship Him as God, in spirit and in truth.

[7] Somewhere doubtless near the walls of the old Jerusalem, or buried under its ruins, is the new sepulchre hewn in the rock where the body of Jesus was laid; but the precise spot, never indicated by the Evangelists, was probably unknown to the next generation, and will in all likelihood remain a matter of doubt always. See Stanley's Sinai and Palestine, p. 149.

[8] Eph. i. 21.

CHAPTER V.

SAMUEL MADE JUDGE OVER ISRAEL.

In the last few chapters has been recorded the history of Israel's sin and Israel's suffering; but no mention has been made of Samuel since his miraculous call in the Temple to be "about his Heavenly Father's business," for the record of Scripture, with this one exception, is entirely silent respecting the earlier days of the ministry of the youthful Prophet. For twenty years, like his Divine antitype, he seems to have remained hid "as the polished shaft in the quiver" of the Lord.

Called, however, as Samuel had been from his youth, and honoured as he had been, by receiving, even as a child, the immediate communications of the Most High, great things must have been expected of one so eminently distinguished; and as "all the house of Israel lamented after the Lord," during the twenty years the Ark abode in Kirjath-jearim, —many of the pious-minded might in this time of their tribulation have said of Samuel, as the disciples said afterwards of Samuel's Lord, "We trusted that it had been he which should have redeemed Israel,"

—but he has left us to ourselves,—he is impotent to save us from the punishment of our sins. The light, however, was behind the cloud, though the heart of the desolate wanted faith to see it. Samuel was interceding for his people, and though "the time was long," the intercession prevailed at last, even as the mightier intercession of Him who afterwards cried, "Father, forgive them, for they know not what they do," will prevail at last, when He who has been the light of us Gentiles shall also hereafter become the glory of His people Israel.

For twenty years the people had been lamenting after the Lord, grieving for their misery without putting away their sin. After the twenty years had elapsed the light began to dawn once more, their hearts began really to soften, and the prophet, who doubtless had watched eagerly for the first symptom of a true and earnest repentance, comes forward at once, exhorts and encourages them. " Samuel spake unto all the house of Israel, saying, If ye do return unto the Lord with all your hearts, then put away the strange gods and Ashtaroth from among you, and prepare your hearts unto the Lord, and serve Him only ; and He will deliver you out of the hand of the Philistines. Then the children of Israel did put away Baalim and Ashtaroth, and served the Lord only. And Samuel said, Gather all Israel to Mizpeh, and I will pray for you unto the Lord. And they gathered together to Mizpeh, and drew water, and poured it out before the Lord, and fasted on that day, and said, We have sinned against the Lord. And Samuel judged the children of Israel in Mizpeh[1]." Thus, then, the people once more returned to the Lord. They prepared their hearts to receive His grace by putting away their idols and by looking *only* to Him. They poured out water as symbolical of this the inward cleansing of their polluted minds; and after a solemn fast, these poor sheep who had gone so sadly astray made their humble and public confession, "We have sinned against the Lord." And as the people had returned to the Lord, He is now to show the truth of His divine promise, that He too will return to them.

The lords of the Philistines, hearing that Israel had assembled at the call of Samuel at Mizpeh, thought it would be a good opportunity to fall upon them and once more to put them to flight; but it is their turn to be utterly discouraged, for though when the Israelites heard of the near approach of the enemy, they were still afraid, yet they turned their hearts to the Lord, and said to Samuel, "Cease not to cry unto the Lord our God for us, that He will save us out of the hands of the Philistines. And Samuel took a lamb, and offered it up *wholly* unto the Lord: and Samuel cried unto the Lord for Israel; and the Lord heard him." The blood of the Lamb with the incense of prayer and supplication was all that Samuel brought that day for the rescue of his people; and while he was in the

[1] 1 Sam. vii. 3—6.

very act of offering up this great typical propitiatory sacrifice, the enemy drew near, and God "thundered upon them from heaven, and they were smitten before Israel," who, pursuing them as conquerors, regained their lost possessions, and drove them entirely from their coast. Thus the land had rest from its enemies, and all was now sunshine in the life of Samuel; God had heard his prayer, and wrought a great deliverance for Israel. Beloved and revered by all, Samuel judged his people with firmness and equity. From year to year he made a circuit to Bethel, and Gilgal, and Mizpeh, and judged Israel in all these places, and his return was to Ramah; for there was his house, and there also he judged Israel. Ever ready to plead for his people, he diligently taught them the right and the good way, and never shrunk from declaring to them the whole counsel of God; he suffered no temporizing with their old sins, and during his time we hear of no idolatrous practices amongst them; his continual superintendence and vigilant care kept the evil in check, and as even the Prophet's eye cannot, like God's, search the very ground of the heart, he might have fondly hoped that the deserved chastisement had worked in them a stable and radical reformation. Inspired with this happy conviction, when after his yearly circuits he returned to his own home at Ramah, no wonder that he built there an altar to the Lord, who had granted his heart's desire and comforted him on every side.

Uninterrupted prosperity however was not to be the portion of this most devoted servant of God. As years went on clouds began to gather around the domestic hearth of the Prophet; like Eli, he was destined to grieve over the unfaithfulness of his children, and affliction was preparing to pierce his bosom with the same arrow which pierced that of the beloved preceptor and guardian of his youth. In Samuel's case, however, the shaft was not poisoned by self-reproach; for as no reproof is uttered against him by the Almighty, we may reasonably conclude that the awful lesson received in childhood was not lost upon him in later years; we may be sure that Samuel taught his sons, as he taught his people, the true and the right way, and that he left no means neglected by which he could train them up in the nurture and admonition of the Lord; and very great indeed were the advantages the Israelites possessed in the early education of their children, for with them, as with us, God's Holy Word was the basis of all their teaching. The law of Moses was to them "not a vain thing, but their life;" the admonitions of the Lord were therefore continually instilled into the youthful mind, "line upon line, precept upon precept, here a little and there a little," thus dropping like the gentle dew from heaven upon the barren and thirsty ground, to develope its latent capabilities, and to fructify the living power which lay concealed in its bosom. In their public services, though no outward image was suffered to attract the eye or captivate the imagination [2], yet the reverence and fear with which their fathers worshipped towards God's Holy Temple must have awed the young mind and filled it with solemn ideas of the Majesty of the Deity. With the Jew also religion was all in all; he found not only his duties, but also his pleasures in the observances of God's holy law [3]. "Rejoice, and again I say unto you, rejoice," was an apostolic exhortation well understood by the pious Israelites; for by coming before the Lord with songs of thanksgiving, by praising Him with their voice as well as with their understanding, by making a cheerful noise to the God of Jacob, by "heartily rejoicing in the strength of their salvation," they taught their children to associate holiness with happiness, the worship of the Creator with the gladness of the creature. Very beautifully, too, were their feasts and festivals calculated to teach the great truths of their holy religion. How practical a lesson of brotherly kindness and charity was given

[2] The "Cherubims of Glory," in the "Holy of Holies," together with all the beautiful things which adorned the "Holy Place," were never exposed to the gaze of the people. While the lights were burning, and the incense breathing, *they* worshipped *without, believing,* but not *seeing,* what was done for them within the veils of the Sanctuary.

[3] The first theatre ever reared on the sacred soil of Judea was built by order of the impious Herod. It rose in the night of their affliction, like a bird of ill omen, to tell of the approaching destruction of that much-loved Sanctuary.

three times in the year when in obedience to the commandment of their God, the master and the children, the manservant and the maidservant, the heathen slave and the stranger, sat down at the festive board, to rejoice together before the Lord and Maker of them all; and when in leafy bowers, with music and with dancing, was commemorated the Feast of the Tabernacles! With what eager animated looks must the young have gathered around the aged, to hear from their lips the wonders that happened to their forefathers in the wilderness where the glorious God brought waters from the rock, and poured down bread from Heaven, when He had been their shadow from the noon-day sun, even as the beautiful foliage above them was at that moment their shadow from its scorching rays! How firmly must all the great events of their history have been fixed in the minds of the listener, how faithfully must they have been transmitted from children to children's children, generation after generation thus bearing witness to the truth of the written Word of God!—a witness which was continued even in their captivity; for while the sorrowing Israelites refused to sing the joyous strains of Zion to those who lightly and cruelly asked of them merriment in their heaviness, yet the fathers to the children still dwelt upon the theme so dear to their hearts, still proclaimed the loving-kindness of the Lord, and the wonders He had done for His chosen people.

In spite, however, of all the external helps afforded by their Ritual, the Hebrew parent had often to learn the utter insufficiency of every safeguard provided by the wisest and most judicious training; he had often to deplore what even the Christian parent has often to deplore; that

> "All these fences, and their whole array,
> One cunning bosom sin blows quite away."

By sad experience the pious Israelite was often made to feel, that, though the culpable weakness of Eli might never be laid to his charge, yet the sinfulness of his children might still be permitted to cloud the bright sunshine of his home, and to embitter the few and evil days of the years of his pilgrimage upon earth.

CHAPTER VI.

SAMUEL CONSECRATES SAUL FIRST KING IN ISRAEL.

UNDER the wise government of Samuel Israel enjoyed great prosperity; they had subdued the Philistines, and even the Amorites were at peace with them. After a time, however, the infirmities of age, and most likely the increasing duties of his office, compelled the Prophet to seek the help of others, as the work was becoming too heavy for him to bear alone.

By the Jewish law, the priesthood was confined to the tribe of Levi[1]; it may be that God, in setting apart for the ministry *one* entire tribe (including both tares and wheat) instead of selecting favoured individuals from each of the tribes of Israel, intended to teach His people that all spiritual blessings shed upon them by the ordinances of the Sanctuary were given, not through the personal righteousness of those who ministered at the altar, but through the mercy of Him, their Heavenly Father.

[1] The tribe of Levi were exclusively devoted to the service of the Temple, under the name of Levites, but of these only the males of the family of Aaron were permitted to sacrifice at the altar of burnt-offering, under the name of *priests*.

Samuel being himself a Levite, his sons were, according to custom, chosen to assist him in his laborious duties. Unfortunately Joel and Abiah did not walk in the way of their father, but turned aside after lucre, and took bribes and perverted judgment; and the Israelites, never sincerely true to their allegiance, but, on the contrary, always but too ready to start aside from their duty, quickly found in the sin of their rulers an excuse for their own disloyalty.

When Hophni and Phinehas desecrated the Temple with their abominable practices, instead of hating the sins of those wicked men, the people deserted the worship of God, and turned their hearts to Baal and Ashtaroth, and now, because Samuel's sons are covetous, they rise up in rebellion against their Heavenly Sovereign, and against their upright, their devoted minister, and their aged judge, one, too, whom they professed to love and to revere; and so deceitful above measure is the human heart, that no doubt they considered the sins of some of those appointed to guide them an all-sufficient excuse for their own ingratitude and disobedience. The elders of Israel, always "blind leaders of the blind," gathered themselves together, and as they knew that there was no use in saying to Samuel, as their forefathers had said unto Aaron, "Make us gods," they said unto him, "Behold, thou art old, and thy sons walk not in thy ways; now make us a king to judge us like the nations." Sorely displeased and distressed at the rebellious spirit manifested by the people, the Prophet sought comfort and help where alone it was to be found. "Samuel prayed unto the Lord;" prayed from the depths of a wounded spirit, agonized by the bitter reflection that the wickedness of his own children had been a stumbling-block in the way of his people, and had induced the flock he had so diligently watched over, so carefully tended, and, as he thought, so successfully trained, to err from the good and right path in which he had led them. He, however, whose eye pierces through all disguises, searching the very ground of the heart, relieved the mind of His servant from this saddest of all reflections, by unveiling to him the true cause of the rebellion of the people. "They have not rejected thee, saith the Lord, they have rejected Me, that I should not reign over them." It was the instability of their own perverse and ungrateful hearts, not the covetousness of the sons of Samuel, which led to this rebellious manifestation: "According to all the works which they have done since the day that I brought them up out of Egypt even unto this day, wherewith they have forsaken Me, and served other gods, so do they also unto thee, saith the Lord." The sin of the people consisted not in their desire to change the form of their government from a theocracy to an earthly monarchy, for a change such as this had been, by anticipation, allowed and provided for in the Book of the Law. The sin of the people consisted in the vain-glorious motive which impelled them to clamour for this change at a time of national peace and prosperity, when the righteous Samuel was their earthly head, and when Jehovah Himself was their all-gracious Sovereign. They sinned in the idolatrous craving of their hearts to be "like unto the heathen;" to have a ruler chosen by themselves; one who would be king by the will of the people, and not by the grace of their God.

In order that we may, in our day, rightly measure the extent of the folly and madness of Israel in rising up against their earthly and their Heavenly Master, we must remember the remarkable position in which they had been placed amidst the nations of the earth ; for, as it had pleased the Almighty to make them, in a peculiar sense, His people, so He had made Himself, in a peculiar sense, their King. He was not only their Lord and Governor— as He had been, is, and ever must be, Lord and Governor of the world—He was their King in a local and exclusive manner; *for them* the Holy of Holies was made His dwelling-place upon earth; *for them* He graciously condescended to open a mysterious, but direct and oral medium of communication through the Urim and Thummim ; *for them* He exercised the prerogatives of an earthly sovereign; He made peace and war, inflicted or remitted punishment, directed, controlled, and regulated the government of His people; they were guided by His omniscience, watched over by His omnipresence, and upheld by His omnipotence [a]. The establishment of the people of God in the Land of Promise was the only realization that has ever been permitted upon earth of the Utopian dream of the enthusiast, for Israel was then but one large brotherhood, all were equal, none were poor; they took possession of goodly cities which they builded not, and houses full of all good things which they filled not, and wells digged which they digged not, vineyards and olive-trees which they planted not; every one of them sat under his own vine and fig-tree, and the land, flowing with milk and honey, was as the Garden of Eden given back once more into the keeping of man. But, alas! it was not a Paradise from which Satan had been expelled, and in which the tree of the knowledge of good and evil had been replaced by that blessed tree whose leaves were for the healing of the nations [b]. It was the old Eden

---

[a] The Jew, though obstinately rejecting the first coming of the Messiah in suffering and humiliation, has never found any difficulty in receiving, literally, the prophetic announcements of the second glorious advent of the "Son of the Blessed," believing, as he has always done, that the Lord God Omnipotent, clad in His vesture of light, in His shining raiment, "exceeding white as snow, so as no fuller on earth can white them," had once, in visible majesty, reigned over His ancient people. The Jew rejects the *past*, but accepts the *future*. It is the maxim of some Christians (says an ancient writer) to reject the *future*, although convinced about the past.

[b] There is no tree of knowledge in the Paradise described to us in the Apocalypse.

with all its loveliness, and, unhappily, with all its seductions. The tempter was there to draw Israel away from its lawful allegiance, and to persuade the people of those days to reject the God who sat between the cherubims, saying, "Make us a king to go before us, that we may be like the heathen," just as in after times he persuaded them to reject the Deity Incarnate in the flesh, saying: "Away with Him! away with Him! we have no king but Cæsar." On both occasions God hearkened to their voice, and let them have their will; on the one, "He gave them a king in His anger," and on the other, "He took him away in His wrath." On this first occasion, however, the Prophet was permitted to assemble the people, to reason with them, to unfold to them the future, and to warn them of all the sorrows, privations, and exactions they were entailing upon themselves and their children. Samuel was to show them that if they thought only of having a warrior to go before them in battle, and to give them consequence in the eyes of the heathen, then they must submit to the evil of a proud and ambitious spirit; if they looked and cared only for the outward appearance of their ruler, then they must be satisfied to forego the higher and more truly valuable qualities of prudence, justice, and wisdom. Thus, commanded by the Lord, faithfully and earnestly did Samuel fulfil his commission. His representations were, however, all in vain. The people had resolved to risk every thing for the grati-

E

fication of their ambition. The final and only answer, therefore, which they gave to the energetic and startling appeal of the Prophet was, "Nay, but we will have a king; that we also may be like the nations, and that our king may judge us, and go before us, and fight our battles[4]." "And the Lord said to Samuel, Hearken unto their voice, and make them a king. And Samuel said unto the men of Israel, Go ye every man unto his city[5]." Thus Samuel sent away the people until it should be revealed to him whom the Lord would choose to be king over Israel.

Incidents in themselves trivial and unimportant were made instrumental in the establishment of the future kingdom of Israel; for though God in the days of old manifested His presence to the multitude by speaking to them in the earthquake, the whirlwind, and the fire, because, unless they "saw signs and wonders, they would not believe," yet to His faithful servants He often spoke in "the still small voice" of the common events of their everyday life, for by *them* little things, as well as great, were received as tokens of His presence, and evidences of His power. They knew that He who had measured the waters in the hollow of His hand, and meted out the heaven with a span, and "comprehended the dust of the earth in a measure, who had stretched out the north over the empty space, and

[4] 1 Sam. viii. 20.   [5] 1 Sam. viii. 22.

hung the earth upon nothing," had also made the mote in the sunbeam, painted the wing of the insect, and clothed the grass which to-day is, and to-morrow is cast into the oven; they knew that He who had raised that wonderful structure, the body of man, had also numbered the very hairs of his head; that He who had designed the beautiful work which was to adorn the mystic veils of His Sanctuary, had also taken thought even for the fringe which was to adorn the garments of its officiating ministers; they knew that He, to whose omnipotence nothing is great, to whose tender consideration nothing is small, was able to make the most trivial circumstances, as well as the most stupendous miracles, alike effectual in working out the good pleasure of His will. Thus, an ordinary domestic occurrence is made, in the Providence of God, the means of bringing to the Prophet the man chosen to be king over Israel.

The father of Saul having lost his asses, the young man had been sent forth to seek them. After searching far and wide, without success, he determined to return to his father, and said to his companion, "Come, and let us return, lest my father leave caring for the asses and take thought for us." The servant, however, unwilling to give up the search, proposes, as a last resource, that they should go into the city to inquire of the man of God, who, by his superior discernment, might peradventure be able to help them out of their difficulty;

and though they were unprovided with a suitable present for the seer, still they determined to persevere. So they both went together, Saul having made up his mind to offer a miserable quarter of a shekel to the man who was about to bestow upon him the gift of a kingdom. The Prophet, forewarned by God that this visit was no accidental occurrence, having satisfied the wanderers as to the safety of the asses, dismissed the servant who accompanied Saul, and communed with the young man long, and we may believe most solemnly, upon the momentous event which was about to raise him to the throne of Israel. Samuel then pours the sacred oil upon the head of the future king, gives him the kiss of peace, and sends him back to his father, who has, indeed, "left caring for the asses, in sorrowing for his son." Furthermore, Saul is commanded to go down before Samuel to Gilgal, there to tarry seven days, at the expiration of which the prophet would meet him to offer burnt-offerings and to sacrifice sacrifices of peace-offerings, "and to tell him what he is to do." Saul and Samuel then part company, the one, to prepare himself for the high destiny which awaits him, and the other, to prepare the people for the reception of their king. At the expiration of the seven days appointed by the prophet, Israel is called together unto the Lord to Mizpeh, and Samuel desires them to present themselves before the Lord, by their tribes, and by their thousands, to receive at his hand the monarch whom God had selected to reign over them. The call was answered at once by the people, but where was the king they had assembled to welcome? he was nowhere to be found. Had he got weary of waiting out the appointed time which the prophet had indicated? Had he doubted the faithfulness of Samuel in fulfilling his promise? No, he had been overcome by a feeling of bashfulness and timidity, most natural to one in his unprecedented position; he had concealed himself so securely from the expectation of the multitude that it required the omnipresent eye of God to indicate where he was to be found. Forcibly drawn from his hiding-place, he was compelled to appear. And when in all the attractiveness of manly beauty, and in all the splendour of a magnificent person, overtopping the most distinguished of his brethren, he met the admiring gaze of the people, and when Samuel, with that noble disinterestedness which is willing to forget itself in order to exalt another, presented him to the multitude, saying, " See ye him whom the Lord hath chosen, that there is none like him among all the people," the stillness of expectation was succeeded by an outburst of enthusiastic delight. In an instant the same prayer was in the heart, and the same words on the lips, of the assembled thousands of Israel, and the hills which compassed Judea were made to resound for the first time in the history of God's people, with one simultaneous loyal and rapturous shout of " God save the king." The

thoughtless multitude, then as now, doubtless used
these words but as a vent to the excited feelings of
the moment; not so, however, were they used by the
prophet of the Lord; in them he recognized a divine
inspiration, given to teach his people, that however
powerful their future monarch might be, he would
owe his greatness to One more powerful than himself;
while, therefore, the voice of Samuel joined heartily in
the outward manifestation of joy with which Israel
welcomed its new-elected monarch, his fervent spirit
arose in prayer to the throne of grace, that God
would indeed " save the king," save him from all the
temptations which would surround his exalted position, save him from pride and ambition, save him
from weakness and folly, save him from the seductions
of pleasure and from the poison of flattery, save him
from the cares and anxieties which make a crown
but a golden sorrow and a heavy weight to the
uneasy head that wears it. On that memorable day
at Mizpeh a new feeling was developed in the minds
of the Israelites; the fire of loyalty for the earthly
sovereign they had been permitted to elect, was
that day kindled in the bosoms of God's ancient
people. We have caught that fire, and with but
temporary intermission, it has burned brightly with
us, and never more brightly than in this our day;
making us, like Israel of old, the most favoured
people amongst the nations of the earth. May this
sacred fire never be suffered to go out on the altar of
our country; may it animate us to endure every

hardship, to face every danger, and, if need be, to lay down our lives in the service of the monarch to whom we have given our allegiance; and may the words with which the Israelites first welcomed their king, continue to be, as they have ever been, *our* words, and their prayer, *our* prayer for the sovereign of these realms, until the fervour of earthly devotion is exchanged for the ecstasy of heavenly adoration, until the enthusiastic shout of assembled thousands is lost in the loud hosannahs of " a multitude which no man can number!"

CHAPTER VII.

SAMUEL TAKES LEAVE OF HIS PEOPLE.

In our last chapter we beheld the Prophet, after having consecrated Saul, affectionately present him to the people of Israel as their future sovereign, with the flattering declaration that there was "none like him among all the people;" and having done this, the Prophet proceeds to regulate the manner in which the new kingdom was to be governed.

"Then Samuel told the people the manner of the kingdom, and wrote it in a book, and laid it up before the Lord." If we turn to the seventeenth chapter of Deuteronomy, we shall find that the omniscience of God had seen, and provided for the important change which had now taken place in Israel, by which His people were henceforth to have an earthly and visible sovereign to reign over them, who was himself to be under the immediate government of the King of kings, and to rule the kingdom strictly according to the laws of the theocracy which He, their Divine Ruler, had established. "When thou art come unto the land which the Lord thy God giveth thee, and shalt possess it, and shalt dwell therein, and shalt say, I will set a king over me, like as all the nations that are about me, thou shalt in anywise set him king over thee whom the Lord thy God shall choose: one from among thy brethren shalt thou set king over thee; thou mayst not set a stranger over thee, which is not thy brother. But he shall not multiply horses to himself, nor cause the people to return to Egypt, to the end that he should multiply horses: forasmuch as the Lord hath said unto you, Ye shall henceforth return no more that way. Neither shall he multiply wives to himself, that his heart turn not away: neither shall he greatly multiply to himself silver and gold. And it shall be when he sitteth upon the throne of his kingdom, that he shall write him a copy of this law in a book out of that which is before the priests the Levites. And it shall be with him, and he shall read therein all the days of his life, that he may learn to fear the Lord his God, to keep all the words of this law and these statutes, to do them: that his heart be not lifted up above his brethren, and that he turn not aside from the commandment, to the right hand or to the left; to the end that he may prolong his days in his kingdom, he, and his children, in the midst of Israel[1]."

The book, then, which Samuel wrote was probably none other than the book of the law of the Lord, which the king was to copy out with his own hand, and in

---

[1] 1 Sam. xvii. 14—20.

which he was to read all the days of his life. Happy would it have been for Saul, and for his people, had this precious book been, indeed, the guide of his life, and the wise and just rule by which he governed his kingdom; he would not then have ascended the dizzy heights of an unscrupulous ambition, and stumbled upon the dark mountains of worldly pride and spiritual presumption! He would have continued as he began, and the blessing of God would then have attended him to the last, as it accompanied him during the first years of his eventful reign, for very soon after his consecration was Saul's prudence, valour, and forbearance to be tested; scarcely had he been proclaimed king before symptoms appeared of murmuring and disaffection. The men of Belial—that is to say, those wild, restless, wicked spirits, ever enemies to peace and all regular government and authority, whether administered by God or by man—rose up against Saul, and tauntingly asked, "How shall this man save us?" The enemy without was not long in profiting by the disunion and disaffection within. Nahash, king of the Ammonites, seized the opportunity, and thought he might insult the men of Jabesh-gilead with impunity, and threaten them with a degree of ferocity beyond what was usual even in those barbarous times; for, to the offer sent by the men of Jabesh to make a covenant with him, the Ammonite answered: "On this condition will I make a covenant with you, that I may thrust out all your right eyes, and lay it for a reproach upon all Israel².". Seven days were given the men of Jabesh to consider this most cruel and degrading proposal, and they sent messengers into all the coast of Israel to see if any help was at hand, for they said to Nahash, "If there be no man to save us, we will come out to thee. Then came the messengers to Gibeah of Saul and told the tidings in the ears of the people, and all the people lifted up their voices and wept."

Surely at this moment conscience must have reproached them for having obstinately determined to exchange their Heavenly King for one powerless as themselves; surely in their inmost hearts they must have been tempted to say of Saul, like the men of Belial, How shall this man save us? How indeed, but through the mediation of the aged ruler they had superseded, and the blessing of the divine Master they had rejected? In this terrible emergency, however, they were not forsaken. It had pleased God to listen to the voice of His people and to give them an earthly sovereign; it was now His pleasure that they should be faithful to the king they had chosen. His Spirit, "without which nothing is strong, nothing is holy," descended upon their king, and Saul said, "What aileth the people that they weep?" And they told him the tidings of the men of Jabesh, and the good Spirit of the Lord came upon Saul and inspired him with promptitude, energy,

² 1 Sam. xi. 2.

and a generous determination instantly to succour the oppressed, and to deliver them from the enemy that so cruelly threatened them; and he took a yoke of oxen, and hewed them in pieces, and sent them throughout the coasts of Israel by the hands of messengers, saying, "Whosoever cometh not forth after Saul and after Samuel (giving honour to the prophet by joining his name to his own), so shall it be done unto his oxen. And the fear of the Lord fell on the people, and they came out with one consent. And when he had numbered them in Bezek, the children of Israel were three hundred thousand, and the men of Judah thirty thousand. And they said unto the messengers that came, Thus shall ye say unto the men of Jabesh-gilead, 'To-morrow, by that time the sun be hot, ye shall have help.' And the messengers came and showed it to the men of Jabesh; and they were glad. Therefore the men of Jabesh said, To-morrow we will come out unto you, and ye shall do with us all that seemeth good unto you. And it was so on the morrow, that Saul put the people in three companies; and they came into the midst of the host in the morning watch, and slew the Ammonites until the heat of the day: and it came to pass, that they which remained were scattered, so that two of them were not left together[s]."

Thus Saul began his reign with a decisive and glorious victory, and the people, ever prone to measure their admiration of their rulers by the

[s] 1 Sam. xi. 6—11.

success which attends them, are now once more enthusiastic about the king they had chosen, and clamour for the lives of the men of Belial who had before despised him, saying, "Who is he that said, Shall Saul reign over us? Bring the men, that we may put them to death." But Saul at this moment shows himself truly great, greater far than when he was conquering the Ammonites, for now he conquers himself, he resists the cry of the people and declares solemnly, " There shall not a man be put to death this day," and then he piously gives the glory of the victory to Him to whom alone it is due. "To-day the Lord hath wrought salvation in Israel!"

Great must have been the joy of Samuel thus to behold the newly elected monarch valiant against his enemies, forgiving towards those who had insulted him, and humble towards his God.

The aged prophet at once seizes this happy moment to engage the people to renew and confirm the kingdom which at one time seemed to be in so precarious and perilous a condition. "Then said Samuel to the people, Come, and let us go to Gilgal, and renew the kingdom there. And all the people went to Gilgal; and there they made Saul king before the Lord in Gilgal; and there they sacrificed sacrifices of peace-offerings before the Lord; and there Saul and all the men of Israel rejoiced greatly[4]."

Having once more with sacrifices and rejoicing

[4]. 1 Sam. xi. 14, 15.

established the kingdom, Samuel feels that it is now his duty to bid his people farewell, and to give up all secular authority over them to their rightful sovereign. He thus, with unaffected simplicity, touchingly addresses them, "Behold, I have hearkened unto your voice in all that ye said unto me, and have made a king over you; and now, behold, the king walketh before you: and I am old and gray-headed; and, behold, my sons are with you: and I have walked before you from my childhood unto this day [5]," and remembering the accusation brought against his sons, he seems peculiarly anxious to clear himself of all participation in their covetous practices and their dishonest love of gain. Having reminded the people that though now old and gray-headed, he had walked before them from a child, he challenges them to say whether he had ever been wanting in his duty, or unfaithful to his trust. This was a severe ordeal, and it is one which a greater than Samuel afterwards went through, for He too condescended to question His ungrateful people, and to ask them, "Which of you convinceth Me of sin?" In the case of the Saviour it was a heathen governor, not one of His own people, who answered the question, saying, I find no fault in Him. In the case of the Prophet, thousands of willing voices in Israel arose to testify to the integrity of Samuel, and in doing so to their own folly and perverseness, in having cast off so mild and gentle a yoke. "And they said,

[5] 1 Sam. xii. 1, 2.

Thou hast not defrauded us, nor oppressed us, neither hast thou taken ought of any man's hand. And he said unto them, The Lord is witness against you, and His anointed is witness this day, that ye have not found ought in my hand. And they answered, He is witness [a]."

Samuel, having thus cleared himself in the sight of the people, as every honest and upright public man ought to do, now for the last time reminds them of all the wonderful acts of the Lord, and of His untiring mercy towards them, in spite of their continual sinfulness in forsaking His worship and disobeying His commands. He then calls for a sign from Heaven, and God sends thunder and rain in wheat harvest, a most remarkable occurrence at that time of the year, and a most significant sign to the people of Israel, for they had just attained all that their ambition craved after; the monarch they had chosen had been crowned with victory, and their enemy had been laid low. All was sunshine within and without, not a cloud was to be seen in the face of Heaven, and universal nature sympathized in the joy of the people, for the fields were ripe for harvest, waiting but the reaper's hand to pour their treasures into the granaries prepared to receive them. But at the word of the Prophet every thing changed; clouds and darkness covered the face of the sky, the tempest approached, the thunder uttered its voice, the ears of corn hung their heavy heads and bent

[a] 1 Sam. xii. 4, 5.

beneath the torrent which came down to overwhelm them—fit emblems of the drooping hearts of the Israelites, for humbled to the dust, and terrified at so unexpected a manifestation of the divine displeasure, they made their confession to the Lord, and implored Him, who had so often before withdrawn the hand lifted up to destroy, once more to pity and to spare His sinful people.

In sending this sign from Heaven the Almighty had shown them how instantaneously He might cut off the staff of life, were He, like themselves, wayward and unstable, and given to change His ordinances, and to alter those laws which in the natural world He had established for their support and security. He had also reminded them of His omnipotence, and in a voice of thunder convinced them that though in the pride and folly of their hearts, they might think to set themselves above His rule and governance, yet most assuredly He would not " deny Himself," nor abdicate in their favour His right of governing a world in which there could be no real power, and no true wisdom but that which came down from Himself, "the Father of Lights," and "the Fountain of all Goodness." Having received their lesson in penitence and submission, God hastens to comfort and to re-assure His trembling children, by saying to the tempest, " Peace, be still," and by giving them, through the mouth of His minister, the cheering assurance of His continued love and providential care.

A last solemn warning against idolatry concludes the Prophet's farewell address to his people: "Yet turn not aside from following the Lord, but serve the Lord with all your heart, and turn not aside: for then should ye go after vain things which cannot profit, nor deliver, for they are vain[7]." How forcibly do these last words of the gray-headed saint of the old dispensation bring to our mind the last words addressed to the general Church of the faithful by the venerable and beloved disciple of the Saviour: "Little children, keep yourselves from idols!"

[7] 1 Sam. xii. 20, 21.

CHAPTER VIII.

SAUL REPROVED BY SAMUEL FOR TAKING UPON HIMSELF THE PRIEST'S OFFICE.

SAMUEL, in his parting address to the people, appears to have given up the secular authority which he had hitherto exercised over them into the hands of the monarch who was now to supply his place; but though in Holy Writ we henceforth hear more of Saul the King than of Samuel the Prophet, the latter continues, nevertheless, to be the support and pillar of the newly-established monarchy. Loyal to his earthly sovereign, and true to his Heavenly Master, the prayer of the righteous was prevailing with God, and a blessing rested for a time upon the people of Israel. Gradually, however, the usual baneful effects of unlimited power and continued earthly prosperity began to work upon the naturally proud and ambitious character of the young monarch. The bright promise which at first he had given of a " King reigning in righteousness, and in the fear of the Lord," seems to have been quickly obscured; for when we again hear the voice of the Prophet, it is not as we last heard it, in accents of hope and encouragement, of exultation and loyalty, but, on the contrary, in accents of reproof and condemnation, for the king had grievously sinned against the Lord; he had taken upon himself the functions of the priesthood, functions which none were permitted to exercise but those who had been regularly called to the ministry. The union, too, of the kingly and priestly office [1] was so strictly forbidden, that the Bible offers no instance in which both these dignities were *lawfully* united in one and the same individual, unless it be that of " Melchisedek, King of Salem, and Priest of the Most High God;" and when we consider how great this man was, "without father, without mother, without descent, having neither beginning of days nor end of life, but made like unto the Son of God," his example could be no precedent, nor could it offer any exculpation of the presumptuous assumption of the king.

The occasion which led Saul to forget himself was as follows. The Philistines and the Israelites were again at war, and just as the latter were preparing to go out against the enemy, Samuel was obliged to absent himself; he had, however, promised to return at the end of seven days, to offer for them the customary sacrifices and burnt-offerings, without which the Israelite never ventured to go forth to battle. During the absence of Samuel, the Philistines had

---

[1] " He shall be a priest upon his throne," was said of "the man whose name is The Branch," *and of no one else.* See Zech. vi

assembled in great force, and the men of Israel saw that they were in a strait. The people, terrified by the formidable preparations of the foe, began, like cowards, "to hide themselves in caves, and in thickets, and in rocks, and in high places, and in pits," and Saul feared (wisely, perhaps, humanly speaking), that unless he rallied them at once, and led them out against the enemy, he should soon be deserted by all his followers, and Israel would become an easy prey to the fierce and bloody Philistine. The king waited the seven days during which the Prophet was to be absent; on the eighth he was to return: no hour, however, had been fixed for that return, so that it might be at even, or at midnight, or it might be delayed to the cock-crowing or the morning[2], and then all would be lost, for every moment was increasing the danger of his position. What, then, was Saul to do? Sacrifice and burnt-offering *must* be offered, and he who alone could legally offer them was away. But, had God, indeed, said that only Samuel could acceptably offer these sacrifices? Was it really true that the efficacy of the offering depended upon the individual appointed to offer it? Were there not other holy men in the camp ready to propitiate the Deity in favour of His people? and might not the Most High Himself see with approval a departure from the strictness of His law? In such an emergency as

[2] It must be remembered that the Jew began his day with the *evening*.

this, where the peril was imminent, and only to be averted by promptness and decision, ought not a ruler to take counsel of his own wisdom, and act for himself? Thoughts such as these might have passed through the mind of the king, and lacking faith to cast the temptation behind him, in an evil moment he forgot that *duties* belong to man, *consequences* to God; and presumptuously he took upon himself the awful responsibility of imposing upon his people a vain and empty ceremony, instead of waiting for the return of the Prophet, who could have offered up for them a true and acceptable sacrifice. The evil servant said in his heart, "My lord delayeth his coming," when, in truth, there was no delay in the matter, for scarcely had the king finished his unrighteous offering when, to his shame and consternation, Samuel appeared. The conscience-stricken monarch, thinking to cover his act of disobedience to God by regal adulation to His minister, on going forth to salute him, is met with the stern and searching interrogation, "What hast thou done?" The king pleads, in extenuation of his sin, the dangers that surrounded him, the alarm of his people, the delay of the Prophet, and declares that he *forced himself* to offer burnt-offering and sacrifice to the Lord. Samuel at once denounces the wickedness of the act by the words, "Thou hast done foolishly," and then goes on to disclose to the king that the trial to which he had been subjected did not come upon him by any accidental combination of circumstances, but had been appointed by God Himself, for the purpose of testing the integrity of his heart, and that upon the issue of the test hung the establishment or the rejection of himself and of his posterity ; so that, had he overcome the temptation, " then (to use the words of Samuel to Saul) would the Lord have established thy kingdom for ever."

In the history of nations, one conscientious or godless act of a legislature may appear to have been the crisis of a people's fate for good or for evil. In the history of an individual, one righteous or faithless act may appear to fix the destiny of that individual for time and for eternity. The biography of the great upon earth abounds in instances perfectly similar to the one recorded for our instruction in the pages of Holy Writ: many a man who, like Saul, has sacrificed the right to the expedient, on looking back upon the past has needed no prophet's voice to sound in his ear, "Thou hast done foolishly," having found, to his cost, that disobedience to the law of God might prove in the end not only a grievous moral transgression, but also a fatal political mistake.

In the case of the king of Israel it may seem hard that an offence committed under peculiarly trying circumstances should have been so severely dealt with ; but was it really for this one offence that he was rejected? or was it not rather for the state of mind which had led him into sin ? By Saul's own confession the voice of conscience had not been silent, nay, so loudly had it spoken, that he had been obliged to exert a power over his mind, he had been obliged to force himself to do foolishly. Why then, instead of thus doing violence to his conscientious scruples, had he not controlled his rash and impetuous spirit? Why, instead of looking forward with dread into the future, had he not sought encouragement by looking back upon the past? Why had he not remembered that once before, at the very same place, even at Gilgal, he had been commanded to wait for seven days the coming of the Prophet, who, true to his word, had on that memorable occasion appeared and presented to his people the monarch they were henceforth to honour and obey? Why had not Saul forced himself to depend upon the friend who had never failed or disappointed him, and upon the God who could make all things, the most adverse, work together for the good of those who put their trust in His mercy? How was it that Saul should have succumbed to a temptation, which in his earlier days he would successfully have resisted and overcome? Assuredly because he had long left off to behave himself wisely, and to walk circumspectly, because he had gradually withdrawn himself from the loyal heart of his best friend and honest adviser, because he had followed the vain imaginations of his heart, and "tampered with the preliminaries of temptation." It is by little and little that the sinner falls, and many are the previous steps that must be taken to bring him to the verge of the precipice, though it is the last fatal step which hurls him to destruction.

In returning to our subject, we read, that Samuel, after having authoritatively condemned the presumptuous act of the king, and prophesied the future uprooting of his dynasty, arose, and departed from Gilgal, while the remnant of the people went up after Saul to meet the enemy, going from Gilgal to Gibeah of Benjamin. Little heeding, it would seem, the rebuke, and disbelieving, we may suppose, the sentence passed against him by the Prophet, the king determined still to rest upon human means, and to put his trust in the arm of flesh. Joining, therefore, his son at Gibeah, he numbered the people, and found himself left with but six hundred men imperfectly armed, to oppose the host of the Philistines, all furnished with swords and spears, and as "the sand on the shore for multitude." In this terrible emergency, Jonathan, one of the most beautiful characters in history, brave as a lion, tender as a dove, "true as the minutes of the watching hour," heroically determined to peril his life in a daring and valiant attempt to discomfit the enemy. Taking to himself the shield of faith, remembering that there is "no restraint to the Lord to save by many or by few," he went forward with his armour-bearer, who, catching the enthusiasm of his youthful commander, put his life into his hand, and followed his leader to death or to victory. By the blessing of the Most High it was to victory; a glorious victory, for the foe was completely routed, and on that day, for the sake of the righteous, the sinner was spared, and Israel was delivered.

This miraculous defeat of the Philistines was followed by a series of great and important victories, for Saul "fought against his enemies on every side, against Moab, and against the children of Ammon, and against Edom, and against the Philistines: and whithersoever he turned himself, he vexed them." Such splendid successes doubtless strengthened the king in self-dependence and wilfulness, and fostered in him the delusive idea that the denunciations of Samuel had been sufficiently disproved. Dismissing, therefore, from his mind all penitential sorrow for the past, and all serious consideration for the future, he appears to have occupied himself entirely in devising means for increasing his resources, and strengthening his internal position, so that he might be enabled to extend his empire, and firmly to establish his dynasty; "every strong man, therefore, and every valiant man" was seized upon to swell the ranks of the army, to strike terror into the minds of his adversaries, and to satisfy the pride and vain-glory of his people. Thus entirely engrossed with projects of ambition and self-aggrandizement, no wonder the word of the Lord was set aside, and the Prophet forgotten by the king.

CHAPTER IX.

SAUL AGAIN REPROVED BY SAMUEL, AND FINALLY REJECTED FROM BEING KING OVER ISRAEL.

IT was said by one who embraced the truths of the Bible with the energies of a powerful intellect, and the reverential feelings of a devout mind [1], that had the history of the kings of England been told as shortly, and with as little preparation for introducing the different events, as the history of the kings of Judah, it would not have been believed in; and most truly may it also be said that, had the history of the kings of Judah been written like the history of the kings of England—had all that has been told been elucidated by all that has been left untold—very few could have believed in it, for very few could have mastered its contents [2]. The sacred

[1] It was the firm persuasion of the same earnest and deep-thinking mind, that knowledge, *truly* so called, could never invalidate the truths of Holy Writ, for upon Boswell telling Johnson of some one who had studied himself into infidelity, the Doctor answered, "Then he must study himself out of it again: drinking largely will sober him."

[2] "How many volumes are there in our library?" asked Ptolemy of his librarian. "Two hundred thousand," answered

history, therefore, was mercifully condensed to meet, not the critical requirements of the rationalist, but the spiritual wants of the faithful; so that, whilst dwelling upon whatever was profitable "for doctrine, for reproof, for correction, for instruction in righteousness," the holy men of old passed over rapidly, and often in total silence, whatever was calculated merely to satisfy the curiosity or to minister to the pride of man. That a succession of writers, from Genesis to the Apocalypse, should, in the manner of their communications, have thus evinced this same oneness of mind, this same singleness of purpose, abundantly proves that "all Scripture was given by the inspiration of God;" that the best witness for the truth of the Bible is to be found in the Bible itself; that "its evidence is involved in its existence."

A very remarkable instance of the brevity of Holy Writ occurs in that portion of the Sacred Record commented upon in the preceding chapter, for one single verse is all the Prophet thinks fit to bestow upon the most brilliant period of the reign of the first king of Israel. In the 47th verse of the 14th

Demetrius, "and I hope soon to make it half a million; for I hear that the Jews have many valuable works in their own language." Happy was it for us that the Sacred Writings would have been but as a drop to the ocean in making up the desired half-million volumes of King Ptolemy's library! happy was it for us that the pious Jew had not to seek after God as the inquiring Greek after wisdom!

chapter, he tells us: "So Saul took the kingdom over Israel, and fought against all his enemies on every side, against Moab, and against the children of Ammon, and against Edom, and against the kings of Zobah, and against the Philistines: and whithersoever he turned himself, he vexed them."

How much of earthly glory is contained in this one single verse, and how long and fondly would the Jewish historian, if left to himself, have dwelt upon the noble deeds of Israel's people and Israel's king! He is not, however, suffered to enlarge upon so congenial a theme; and though many important events, independently of these numberless victories, must have happened in the time which intervened between the 14th and 15th chapters, nothing more is told us either of Saul or of Samuel, until, as the ambassador of the Most High, the Prophet stands again in the presence of the king; for God, who willeth not the destruction, but the reformation of the sinner, had been pleased once more to lay His commands upon His erring servant, and to give him an opportunity of restoration to His favour.

The Prophet, before he delivers the message with which he had been charged, anxious, it would seem, to recall the king to a sense of the duty of subjection to Divine authority, and also of his responsibilities as the leader of God's people, begins by reminding him who it was that first called him to his high position, and who it was that had consecrated him king over Israel. "Now, therefore (continues the Prophet), hearken thou unto the voice of the words of the Lord." "Thus saith the Lord of Hosts, I remember that which Amalek did to Israel, how he laid wait for him in the way, when he came up from Egypt. Now go and smite Amalek, and utterly destroy all that they have, and spare them not; but slay both man and woman, infant and suckling, ox and sheep, camel and ass [3]."

Saul had already fought against the Amalekites and partially subdued them, but now he is enjoined not to spare but entirely to exterminate them. The command was terrible in its awful severity, but it was given by God Himself; and we may, therefore, be quite sure, that it was no cruel purpose which influenced the Almighty to bring to an end the abominable wickedness of the parents, to take the children to Himself, and to transplant the tender suckling from a polluted earthly soil to the nurseries of Heaven.

When we read in the Bible of these sweeping exterminations, we must never forget that they were exceptional in the history of the Jew; for *then*, as *now*, mercy was God's delight, whilst judgment was His strange work [4].

[3] 1 Sam. xv. 1—3.
[4] The Jewish people were never cruel or blood-thirsty,—torture, that fearful political engine so freely used by heathen, and, alas! by Christian governments, was unknown to the Jew—he suffered from it, but he never inflicted it. "Forty

Noble and generous natures are invariably tender-hearted; so we can imagine that the carrying out of such terrible inflictions must have been very grievous to the compassionate heart of a Joshua, and a sore trial of his faith and obedience; but to the man who once would have sacrificed without pity the life of his own son, and who seemed ever reckless of the sufferings of his subjects where his own ambitious projects were concerned,—a command which held forth the promise of a glorious and decisive victory over one of the fiercest of the foes of Israel, would seem to have so completely harmonized with his thirst of conquest and love of power, as to have precluded any trial of his faith, or any exercise of his obedience. Indeed, the alacrity with which the king gathers the people together, and prepares himself at once for the execution of the great work which he had been commissioned to carry out, would lead us to believe, that, this time at least, he would not be found wanting in the strict fulfilment of his duty, since duty and inclination would so entirely agree. But, alas! such was not the case. "The spirit which *now* worketh in the children of disobedience" worked

stripes save one," was the limit of corporal punishment permitted by their law, and when in a paroxysm of fury they sought to inflict an excruciating death upon the meek and lowly Saviour of the world, they were compelled to have recourse to the highly cultivated and civilized Roman: crucifixion being not a Jewish but a Roman invention for prolonging the agonies of criminals condemned to death.

then in the mind of Saul, and led him to stop short in the righteous performance of God's commandment, and to seek and to find some way of showing that to do his own will, not God's will, was the mainspring of his actions, and the chief purpose of his life.

Nothing could have been clearer or more decided than the command given to the king utterly to destroy the sinners the Amalekites. He chose, however, to think for himself, and to evade the strict fulfilment of the duty imposed upon him. In leaving undone a portion of the work which God had given him to do, was Saul arrested by the cries of the women, by the wail of the infant and the suckling? Was it *here* that his heart failed him and his resolution faltered?—no such tender weakness, no such mistaken, but still compassionate, feeling could be pleaded in extenuation of the disobedience of the king. This part of the work he executed rigorously and effectually; nothing had been spared, all the people had been slain with the edge of the sword, and every thing that was vile and refuse, *that* they had destroyed utterly; but Agag, the king of the Amalekites, he who had been the terror of the nations around him, from his abominable cruelty, and a scourge to his people by training them to violence and crime, he had been taken alive and spared by the conqueror,—not, it must be believed, from pity to the fallen, but from the ambitious desire of having the captive monarch to grace his triumph, and to be a living evidence of the victory his arms had achieved. The best of the sheep, too, and the oxen, and of the fatlings, and the lambs, and all that was good, was spared under the hypocritical pretence of sacrificing to the Lord.

Very quickly must the public voice of joy and thanksgiving have brought to Samuel the glorious tidings of the defeat of the Amalekites; but the Prophet was precluded from sympathizing in the joy, or from joining in the thanksgiving of his people, God having made known to him the sin which had clouded the brightness of the triumph; the unfaithfulness which had turned that victory into defeat. Wonderful and painful must have been the contrast which on that eventful occasion presented itself to the mind of the Prophet; on the one hand, he listened to the enthusiasm of the multitude singing the praise of him who had again "his thousands slain," on the other, to the denunciations of the offended Deity, proclaiming the transgression of the victor, and his final expulsion from the throne of Israel; for "the word of the Lord came unto Samuel, saying, It repenteth Me that I have set up Saul to be king: for he is turned back from following Me, and hath not performed My commandment. And it grieved Samuel; and he cried unto the Lord all night." All night the Prophet poured forth his soul in supplication to his God, too loyal and devoted to "suffer his eyes to sleep, or his eyelids to slumber, or the temples of his head to take any rest," while a hope remained that he might avert from his sinful, but much-loved sovereign, the heavy displeasure of his God. The heart knoweth its own bitterness, and the mental suffering of that sad vigil was seen only by Him to whom this fervent and prolonged but ineffectual intercession was addressed; for though the morning dawned upon the sleepless eye of the Prophet, no hope dawned on his heart that his prayer had been accepted; on the contrary, he is commanded to arise from the earth, to go forth in obedience to his Heavenly Master, and bear to the king the irrevocable sentence of rejection from the Lord.

It was at Gilgal, that fatal Gilgal, that Samuel again met the conqueror returning from the field of battle elated with his recent successes, little thinking of the cloud so soon to burst in anger upon his head. The sovereign, as usual, welcomes the Prophet with words of reverence and piety, " Blessed art thou of the Lord," followed by an eager declaration of his own integrity, " I have performed the commandment of the Lord."

Those who stand at the right hand of the Throne of Glory on the last dread day of account are represented as having entirely forgotten their labours of love, and those on the left, their sins of omission: the king of Israel by his false and daring assertion seems, like these latter unprofitable servants, to have altogether forgotten that the rebellious spirit manifests itself not only in what is done, but also in what is left undone. Sounds in the distance, contradicting the declaration of the king, met the ear of the Prophet, for Samuel said unto Saul, "What meaneth then this bleating of the sheep in mine ears, and the lowing of the oxen which I hear? And Saul said, They have brought them from the Amalekites: for the people spared the best of the sheep and the oxen, to sacrifice unto the Lord thy God; and the rest we have utterly destroyed." Saul, to excuse himself, accuses his people, just as if a people on all other occasions so entirely submissive to his despotic sway, would not have been equally submissive on this occasion also, had their ruler been as faithful in exacting obedience to the Divine will, as he had ever been rigorous in carrying out his own. This ungenerous conduct on the part of Saul presents a striking contrast to the noble self-devotion of his illustrious successor, who, when he beheld the avenging angel in Heaven, armed with the terrors of judgment against his people, went forth alone to meet the storm, with the language of self-condemnation on his lips, and the earnest prayer that its fury might be spent upon himself and his father's house, that so it might altogether be turned aside from the poor sheep of his pasture.

The Prophet, entirely disregarding the excuses of the king, proceeds at once to deliver the message of the Lord. Then Samuel said unto Saul, "Stay, and I will tell thee what the Lord hath said to me this night. And Saul said unto him, Say on. And Samuel said, When thou wast little in thine own sight, wast thou not made the head of the tribes of Israel, and the Lord anointed thee king over Israel? And the Lord sent thee on a journey, and said, Go, and utterly destroy the Amalekites, and fight against them until they be consumed. Wherefore, then, didst thou not obey the voice of the Lord, but didst fly upon the spoil, and didst evil in the sight of the Lord*?" Here Saul reiterated his former assertion, and solemnly declared that it was the people who had sinned. "For Saul said unto Samuel, Yea, I have obeyed the voice of the Lord, and have gone the way which the Lord sent me, and have brought Agag, the king of Amalek, and have utterly destroyed the Amalekites. But the people took of the spoil, sheep and oxen, the chief of the things which should have been utterly destroyed, to sacrifice unto the Lord thy God in Gilgal. And Samuel said, Hath the Lord as great delight in burnt-offerings and sacrifices, as in obeying the voice of the Lord? Behold, to obey is better than sacrifice, and to hearken than the fat of rams⁶."

The sacrifices of the law were divinely instituted as means by which the faith of God's people was to be tried, their obedience exercised, and their hope kept alive in the coming of the true Paschal Lamb, "the Lamb of God, which taketh away the sin of the world," and with this faith and obedience, even "the

* 1 Sam. xv. 16—19.   ⁶ 1 Sam. xv. 20, 21.

blood of bulls and of goats, and the ashes of an heifer, sprinkling the unclean, sanctified to the purifying of the flesh." Without this faith and obedience, all the rich flocks and herds of the Amalekites were utterly worthless in the sight of God. We therefore find that, though these sacrifices were imperatively exacted, and so awful in their sanctity that no unauthorized hand was to offer them, no strange fire was to consume them ; yet, when rested in, and considered as efficacious in themselves, and not as shadows of good things to come, they were declared by prophet after prophet not only to have lost all their value, but to have become positively an abomination in the sight of the Lord. Holy men of old, speaking as they were moved by the Holy Ghost, testified with wonderful unanimity to this great truth [7]. In Micah we read: " Will the Lord be pleased with thousands of rams, or with ten thousand rivers of oil? He hath showed

---

[7] This wonderful unanimity is an internal evidence to the divine inspiration of the Old Testament Scriptures, which no sophistry can invalidate. Well and truly has it been said, that, though in the spirit of a miserable criticism, ministering to a still more miserable philosophy, we evacuate the Old Testament of every express miracle it records, though we make our Elijahs and Isaiahs pretenders to power and conjecturers in knowledge—and, it might have been added, our Samuels impostors—we cannot, even so, clear the Old Testament of wonders. We may deny the story of the miracles, but we cannot destroy the miracle of the story. *We cannot un-miracle the obstinate fact of the Volume itself.*

thee, O man, what is good; and what doth the Lord require of thee, but to do justly, to love mercy, and to walk humbly with thy God?" In Amos: "I hate, I despise your feast days, and I will not smell in your solemn assemblies; though ye offer Me burnt-offerings and your meat-offerings, I will not accept them; neither will I regard the peace-offerings of your fat beasts." In Hosea: "I desired mercy, and not sacrifice; and the knowledge of God more than burnt-offerings." In Jeremiah: "When they fast I will not hear their cry; and when they offer burnt-offering and an oblation, I will not accept them." In Isaiah: "To what purpose is the multitude of your sacrifices unto Me? saith the Lord; I am full of the burnt-offerings of rams, and the fat of fed beasts; and I delight not in the blood of bullocks, or of lambs, or of he-goats. Bring no more vain oblations." In the Psalms: "I will take no bullock out of thy house, nor he-goat out of thy folds; for every beast of the forest is Mine, and the cattle upon a thousand hills. Will I eat the flesh of bulls, or drink the blood of goats? Offer unto God thanksgiving; and pay thy vows unto the Most High." And in Samuel: "To obey is better than sacrifice, and to hearken than the fat of rams. For rebellion is as the sin of witchcraft, and stubbornness is as iniquity and idolatry."

Did coming events cast their shadows before them, and did the far-seeing eye of the Prophet anticipate how exactly his words would be verified in the downward career of him to whom they were addressed? Did Samuel foresee how truly in the case of Saul rebellion would lead to a sinful tampering with the power of darkness, and stubbornness to the iniquity and idolatry of turning to the creature instead of trusting in the Creator? If such were the forebodings of the man of God, with what mournful solemnity must he have pronounced the final condemnation of the chosen of the people, the first monarch of Israel! "Because thou hast rejected the word of the Lord, He hath also rejected thee from being king." On hearing these words, the stout heart of the sinner seemed to have forsaken him, and the consequence of the divine displeasure to have, for a moment, excited his apprehension; for he said unto Samuel, "I have sinned, for I have transgressed the commandment of the Lord and thy words, because I feared the people, and obeyed their voice; now, therefore, I pray thee pardon my sin, and turn again with me, that I may worship the Lord." And Samuel said unto Saul, "I will not return with thee, for thou hast rejected the word of the Lord, and the Lord hath rejected thee from being king over Israel." After reiterating the condemnation of the king, the man of God, glad, we may be sure, to put an end to a scene so harrowing to the feelings of his heart, turned about to leave the royal presence, when Saul, in order forcibly to detain him, laid hold of the skirt of his mantle, but, alas! no virtue went out of it to heal the sin-sick soul, for it rent in his hand, and became a sign that the Lord had rent the kingdom of Israel from his grasp, and given it to one more worthy than himself. Saul, still passionately clinging to earthly thoughts and earthly desires, vehemently urges the Prophet to turn with him to worship the Lord, and to honour him before the elders of his people. The melancholy thought might, perhaps, have crossed the mind of the Prophet, that never again would he be called upon to do homage to his sovereign, for his resolution gives way, and Samuel turned after Saul, and, for the last time, he honours the king in the presence of his people.

One imperative duty remained to be fulfilled: the sentence of the Lord must be carried out against the King of Amalek, for no spurious compassion inclined the man of God to spare the guilty at the expense of the innocent, "to murder mercy, by letting the murderer go free." The sword, therefore, which had so long, without pity, made mothers childless, must now make childless the mother of Agag [a].

The prayer of Deborah, at the destruction of Sisera, might have been the prayer of Samuel at the fall of the King of Amalek: "So let Thine enemies perish, O Lord; but let them that love

---

[a] It is said that to hew in pieces the poor victims who fell into his power was the favourite pastime of this Nana Sahib of ancient days.

him be as the sun when he goeth forth in his might."

The Prophet, in witnessing, or in carrying out the execution of Agag, acted under the immediate direction of the Almighty. Even in this terrible act of retributive justice, he was a type of Him who is represented as saying hereafter to the ministers of his wrathful indignation, "Those Mine enemies, which would not that I should reign over them, bring hither and slay them before Me [9]."

"Is God unrighteous, who taketh vengeance? (I speak as a man.) God forbid! for then how should God judge the world [10]?"

[9] Luke xix. 27.   [10] Rom. iii. 5, 6.

CHAPTER X.

SAMUEL COMMANDED TO CONSECRATE DAVID.

AFTER the events of the preceding chapter we are told that Samuel returned to his home at Ramah, and Saul "went up to his house at Gibeah," and that Samuel came no more to see Saul until the day of his death, but that, nevertheless, Samuel mourned for Saul. In spite of the king's ingratitude, in spite of his continued neglect and desertion, nay, in spite of the vindictive malice and hatred which made the wretched monarch seek even the life of the Prophet, nevertheless Samuel mourned for Saul. He mourned for the Saul of other and better days; for he remembered that at Mizpeh the valour of the warrior had excited the admiration of his people, whilst the humility of a servant of God had satisfied the heart of the Prophet; that at Jabesh-gilead the noble disinterestedness of a generous mind had made head against the popular voice, and saved his enemies from the fury of the people, ascribing not unto himself, but unto the Lord, the victory he had achieved.

The Prophet looked back upon the past, and

Samuel mourned for Saul, and yet the Saul for whom Samuel mourned was at that very moment at the zenith of all human prosperity, of all earthly glory, in the vigour of manhood, with all his physical and intellectual faculties about him; he was feared and admired by his people, for they saw in the ruler they had chosen one who had exalted the glory of Israel in the sight of the heathen. In the true-hearted Jonathan, who, to the noble qualities of the hero, united the virtues of the saint, the king had a worthy successor to his throne, and other goodly sons were also given him, to ensure the succession and to continue his dynasty. At that moment, too, the King of Israel had, by a great and decisive victory, laid low, for ever, the fiercest of the foes of Israel; and yet, in spite of all this greatness, and all this glory, " Samuel mourned for Saul," for he looked beyond the idle pageantry of this world, he looked beyond the passing sunshine which seemed to gild with the brightness of its rays the throne of the king, and he saw the dark speck, the little cloud which would spread and spread, until gradually covering the horizon, it would hide from the ill-fated monarch the sun of prosperity and the countenance of his God. The Prophet saw that he who was then like a proud cedar of Libanus, with fair branches, and a shadowing shroud, and of an high stature, with his top among the thick boughs, " so great, so glorious, as to be the envy of all the trees of Eden that grow in the garden of

God," would, nevertheless, be driven out for his wickedness, and delivered into the hands of the "mighty one of the heathen;" and, "because his heart had been lifted up in his height, would be brought to the nether parts of the earth, and made to lie down in the midst of the uncircumcised, with them that had been slain with the sword." Samuel mourned for Saul, for he knew that the word of the Lord had gone forth against the king, and he also knew that nothing could now avert the last sad catastrophe which would lay the proud spirit in the dust. The Prophet is so often represented as the stern and uncompromising bearer of the denunciations of the Most High, that, had not the secret workings of that true and honest heart been laid bare before us; had we not been told how, as a child, the youthful spirit failed him in telling Eli the vision; had not that agonizing vigil been revealed to us, in which all night he had cried unto God, and pleaded for the sinner; had it not now been revealed to us how long and deeply he mourned for Saul; we might have been tempted to look upon the Prophet as an austere man, likely to inspire fear, but never to win the love of those with whom he had to do. We might have ignorantly supposed him to have been wanting in that sympathetic tenderness for the sorrows of others, indispensable in one represented to us as a perfect type of Him who in all our afflictions was afflicted, who bare our griefs, and who carried our sorrows. Samuel mourned for Saul, and so long and so deeply did he mourn that, for once, the voice of God, hitherto so loving, so gentle to the ear of His servant, is heard in accents of reproof and displeasure. For the word of the Lord came unto Samuel, saying, "Wilt thou not cease to mourn for Saul, seeing that I have rejected him from being king over Israel?" God, who is all tenderness to the natural affections which He has Himself implanted in the heart of His creatures, who wills that men should grieve as well as rejoice, had mercifully considered the feelings of His servant, and given him a time to mourn; but it would seem from the sacred narrative that the mourning of Samuel, by its long continuance, and its excessive indulgence, was in danger of assuming an aspect of heart-rebellion against the dispensations of the Most High. It seemed as if the Prophet, in his love for his earthly sovereign, was in danger of forgetting that higher allegiance which he owed to the will of his God. He must, therefore, be called back to his duty. He must now cease to mourn for Saul; he must depose the sinner from the throne of his heart, and he must open that heart to receive the successor whom God had appointed. "Fill thine horn with oil, and go. I will send thee to Jesse, the Bethlehemite, for I have provided Me a king among his sons." Oh, how weak is man when governed by his affections! for though this command is given by God Himself, though Samuel had never before refused to brave the anger of the king, and to encounter every danger in doing the bidding of the Lord, yet now he falters, hesitates, and seeks for some plausible excuse, some good reason why he may draw back from fulfilling a mission which he feels altogether repugnant to the love, still so strong in his bosom, for the monarch he is thus called upon to supersede. He pleads that, should Saul hear of his having anointed his successor, he would infallibly take his life: "How can I go? If Saul hear it, he will kill me." This objection is at once set aside; for he is told that it is not the will of God that the anointing of the future king of Israel should be made public, or that Saul should hear of it. For the Lord said unto Samuel, "Take a heifer with thee to Bethlehem, and say, I am come to sacrifice to the Lord, and call Jesse to the sacrifice, and I will show thee what thou shalt do; and thou shalt anoint unto Me him whom I name unto thee[1]." All suspicion as to the real importance of the Prophet's mission to Bethlehem is thus to be avoided, not, assuredly, because it was necessary for Him who, with a word, can still the "raging of the sea, and the noise of his waves, and the madness of the people," to adopt any thing like a subterfuge to secure the safety of His servant; but in thus arranging His providential designs, God reveals Himself to us as working in secret, through the instrumentality of the ordinary events of His pro-

[1] 1 Sam. xvi. 3.

vidence, events too common to excite the hopes or fears of His creatures; thus teaching us that though "His way is in the sea, and His paths in the great waters, and His footsteps are not known;" that though "all things remain as they were from the beginning of the creation;" that though "seed-time and harvest succeed each other, and the fig-tree puts forth its leaves in due season, and the other trees their blossom;" that, in spite of all this seeming tranquillity, the Most High is carrying on behind the veil of these, His ordinary providences, the wonderful designs of futurity, and will suddenly, at an hour when they least expect it, call upon the righteous to rejoice that their redemption draweth nigh, and upon the wicked to tremble at the judgments which are coming upon the world. The heart of the Prophet had shrunk for a moment from the office he was called upon to perform, but the right spirit within him very quickly resumed its legitimate influence, and made him ready to yield up his own will to the will of his Heavenly Father. Accordingly, without any further delay, he fills his horn with oil, takes the heifer which is to be offered in sacrifice upon the consecration of the future king of Israel, and thus prepared, he leaves Ramah for Bethlehem, in implicit obedience to the Divine command.

CHAPTER XI.

SAMUEL CONSECRATES DAVID AT BETHLEHEM TO BE KING INSTEAD OF SAUL.

THE visit of Samuel caused no little stir amongst the people of Bethlehem; "the elders of the town trembled at his coming, and going forth to meet him, they said unto him, Comest thou peaceably? and he said, Peaceably,"—peaceably as his great predecessor went into Egypt to deliver his people from the bondage of Pharaoh; peaceably as his Divine prototype came afterwards to that very Bethlehem to deliver the world from the bondage of Satan; so peaceably did the Prophet now come to the birthplace of Jesse, with no sword but God's word, no shield but the protection of the Almighty. Having thus announced his mission to be one of peace and good will, the elders of Bethlehem are invited to the great sacrifice which is to be offered up unto the Lord. The Prophet also sanctified Jesse and his sons for the approaching ceremony, and upon looking on the elder-born of Jesse, who was tall in stature and very strikingly handsome, the image of the still beloved Saul, when in manly beauty he out-topped his fellows at Gilgal, seems to have risen up before the mind's eye of the Prophet. The man of God, misled by the feelings of his heart, looked lovingly on Eliab, and said, "Surely the Lord's anointed is before Him. But the Lord said unto Samuel, Look not on his countenance, or on the height of his stature; because I have refused him: for the Lord seeth not as man seeth; for man looketh on the outward appearance, but the Lord looketh on the heart[1]." Seven of the sons of Jesse were made one after the other to pass before the Prophet, and Samuel said to Jesse, " The Lord hath not chosen these." Not one of these seven sons was the chosen one of Israel. But where was the eighth, that there seemed to be no room for him in his father's house? where was the youngest-born of Jesse, that he seemed thus cast out, set at nought, passed over, and altogether forgotten? The Prophet, perplexed and disappointed at the rejection of those presented to him, questions Jesse as to whether *all* his sons had been made to pass before him, and receives for answer, that there remaineth yet the youngest, and, behold, said Jesse, " he keepeth the sheep." He, the good shepherd, was tending those "poor sheep in the wilderness," for the care of which he was willing to bear the taunts and scoffs of the scorner Eliab, and for the love of which he had been found ready boldly to face the lion and

---

[1] 1 Sam. xvi. 7.

the bear, to pluck the feeble lamb from the very jaws of destruction, to encircle it in his loving arms, and to bear it back once more in triumph to the fold. The Prophet on being told that there remaineth yet another son of the house of Jesse, made known his determination not to sit down to the festive board, until David was there to grace it. The keeper of the sheep, therefore, is diligently sought after, on mountain top or in lowly vale, and being found, is brought back to his home, and presented to the Prophet; and though there is no striking beauty in him as in Saul and Eliab to attract and captivate the outward senses, yet he is described in the sacred record as "goodly to look upon," with a countenance irradiated by the inspirations of the poet, and beautiful in its expression of goodness and of piety. No sooner does David appear than the word of the Lord came to the Prophet, saying, "This is he."

How many thoughts of reverence and gratitude arise in the mind of the Christian on listening to the simple words of this divine announcement, remembering that "this is he," not only so illustrious as king, warrior, and prophet, but "this is he" also, who has made the whole creation vocal with the praises of Him who spake and it was done, who commanded and it stood fast; "this is he" whose voice has been heard in all lands, and whose words have gone forth to the ends of the world, who has provided a prayer for every woe, a thanksgiving for every blessing, and whose name has been so honoured as to be the one earthly name linked in Holy Writ to that only Name under Heaven by which we may be saved: for it is not as the Son of Abraham, not as the Son of Joseph, not as the Son of Mary, but as the "Son of David," that the Christian is permitted to invoke his Redeemer, and to implore the mercy of his God.

"And the Lord said unto Samuel, Arise, and anoint him, for this is he." "And Samuel took the horn of oil, and anointed him in the midst of his brethren."

Thus, in the town of Bethlehem of Judea, "not the least among the princes of Judah," and in the humble dwelling of Jesse, in the absence of all external pomp and circumstance, in stillness and in secrecy was accomplished the most important event recorded in the history of God's ancient people, the consecration of David to be king over Israel. No tidings of this event were suffered to reach the ear of his proud and implacable enemy; no invisible hand went forth to write in fiery characters upon the palace-walls of the king of Israel, that he had been weighed in the balance and found wanting; no assembled thousands were gathered together at Bethlehem, to greet their newly-elected sovereign, and make the hills around Jerusalem reverberate once more with the long and enthusiastic shout of "God save the King." On the elevation of one whose seed was "to endure for ever," and whose throne was "to be as the days of Heaven," there might have been hosannahs above, but there were none upon earth to startle Saul from his fancied security. All things remained the same so far as the sinner was concerned. The sun was shining upon him as brightly as ever, his people were as ready as ever to bow down before him, his warriors as ready as ever to risk their lives in his service, his authority remained as unquestioned, and his power as unlimited as ever; and yet, it was nevertheless true that the king of Israel had that day been superseded by one more worthy than himself, and that the word of the Lord had definitively gone forth against him, saying, "Take off the diadem; remove the crown." And, not only did Saul remain in utter ignorance of the consecration of David, but even Jesse, and the other sons of Jesse, seem to have been as unconscious as Saul of the dignity which Samuel had just conferred upon one of their house and lineage, and of the exalted position which David was to occupy, for "neither did his brethren believe in him," none of them suspecting that his word would be their law, and that to him they would hereafter be compelled to bow the knee in reverence and submission. But was the Prophet also without understanding? Was Samuel, when he poured the oil on the youthful head of the shepherd of Israel, was he also unable to realize the important nature of the ceremony he had been called upon to perform? This evident reluctance to undertake the sacred mission, the mistake he was about to make in the choice of Eliab, his ignorance as to the person and even as to the existence of David, lead us to the conclusion that Samuel merely saw in the lowly stem of Jesse, a successor to Saul, and one, perhaps, who, like Saul, might die in his sins, and whose dominion, like Saul's, might be overthrown by the righteous judgments of his God. We know that to the Prophet was revealed the mighty salvation which God was preparing for His people, and that, like the other holy men of old, "he saw afar off the sufferings of Christ, and the glory that should follow." But we also know, from the record of Holy Writ, that the saints of the Lord were first called upon to walk in the obedience of faith, before they were permitted to rejoice in the vision of salvation. It was after the patriarch Job had endured the extreme of human suffering, without "charging God foolishly," that he was permitted to "see with the eye" the gracious Being of whom he had before heard only "by the hearing of the ear."

It was when Abraham had yielded up Isaac, at the bidding of the Almighty, that in the Mount of the Lord it was given him to see [2] that God had indeed provided Himself a Lamb for a burnt-offering [3], and laid upon it the iniquity of us all.

It was after a night of mysterious wrestling with

---

[2] See Gen. xxii. 7—14, and John viii. 56.   [3] Gen. xxii. 8

"a man" whom he knew not, that "the day broke" for the patriarch Jacob, and the Sun of righteousness arose upon him with healing on his wings, for as a prince he had prevailed with God and man; "he had seen God face to face, and his life had been preserved to him." It was when Moses had fulfilled the mission entrusted to him, and had brought his people out of Egypt, and from the house of bondage, that God, instead of showing him His glory, made "all His goodness to pass before him." It was after Joshua had led Israel over the Jordan, and, trusting to the Divine protection, had ventured into the midst of an enemy, fierce, powerful, and warlike, that he was privileged to look upon "the captain of the host of the Lord," the great Captain of his salvation, and to realize in Him the presence of the Deity, by the solemn injunction, "Loose thy shoe from off thy foot, for the place whereon thou standest is holy;" and thus it might have been with Samuel. It might have been after he had broken the last tie which bound him to the earth, and at the bidding of the Most High had deposed the monarch he had clung to with such unswerving loyalty, such devoted affection, that God might have comforted His servant by a full revelation of the glories of that kingdom of Judah, of which the son of Jesse was to be the earthly founder, and of whom "as concerning the flesh" the Shiloh, the peaceful one, the true "man after God's own heart, David's root and David's branch," David's son and David's Lord, should come, not to abolish or to exterminate the kingdom of His great progenitor, but " to order and to *re-establish it* with justice and with judgment for ever, and *beginning at Jerusalem* " to extend it from sea to sea, and from the river to the ends of the earth, " bringing his people from the east, and gathering them from the west, saying to the north, Give up; and to the south, Keep not back [4]." " Enlarge the place of thy tent, and let them stretch forth the curtains of thine habitations: spare not, lengthen thy cords, and strengthen thy stakes; for thou shalt break forth on the right hand and on the left; and thy seed shall inherit the Gentiles, and make the desolate cities to be inhabited [5];" thus fulfilling the oath sworn unto Abraham, and the promise made to Sarah, that she should be the mother of nations, and that kings of peoples should be born of her, kings who should worship, and nations who should serve, Him whose dominion was an everlasting dominion, and whose kingdom that which should never be destroyed. As one whom his mother comforteth, so must the Prophet have been comforted, if permitted to see that though the beautiful vine of Israel, which he had so lovingly tended, would one day be made desolate, its hedges broken down, and its branches plucked off, though the boar out of the wood would waste it, and the

---

[4] See Isa. xliii. 5, 6.   [5] Isa. liv. 2, 3.

wild beast of the field devour it, yet that still a cluster would remain, for a blessing would be in it, and a branch would be spared to take root downwards and to flourish upwards, and once more to fill the earth with its fruit*, and to cover it with its goodly shadow. Oh, what happiness for the large and disinterested heart of the Prophet, to feel that his labours would not be in vain in the Lord, and that others would enter into those labours, and reap what he had sown, and that though he without them could not be made perfect, they without him would have been incomplete! How must it have cheered the man of God to behold the "star of Jacob" shining through the darkness which would cover his people, and to see the sceptre of Judah still grasped by a hand not shortened that it could not save, and to know that in her deepest humiliation "the shout of a king" would still be in her, and that the "Lion of the tribe of Judah, the root of David," would never be more able to manifest His power than when He "stooped down," never more terrible to rouse than "when He couched," and laid His glory prostrate in the dust! How intense must have been the interest of the Prophet, if permitted to watch the increase of that "day of small things" which had just dawned upon him at Bethlehem, and to see the progress of that blessed kingdom, which, like the little stream issuing at first from the fissure of

* See Isa. xxvii. 6.

the rock, would widen into a glorious river, vivifying the parched and thirsty ground, making the wilderness and solitary place to be glad, and the desert to rejoice and blossom as the rose, and pursuing its course through all time and all space, would "cover the earth with the knowledge of the glory of God as the waters cover the sea," and having finished its course, having done the work it was appointed to do, would in the end reunite itself to the unfathomable ocean from which it issued, and to which it must return'! If permitted fully to realize these all-momentous and blessed results of the consecration of David to his own people Israel, as well as to all the nations of the earth, not only must the Prophet have ceased to mourn for Saul, but he must at once have exchanged "the spirit of heaviness for the garment of praise," he must have rejoiced with joy unspeakable and full of glory. He must have felt as if the important ceremony, which in his sacred office he had been called upon to perform, ought to be, as in truth it was, the appropriate termination of his long and eventful career.

' See 1 Cor. xv. 24, 28.

CHAPTER XII.

THE DEATH OF SAMUEL.

THE consecration of David was the last important ministerial act recorded in Scripture which Samuel, as Prophet of the Lord, was called upon to perform. From his home at Ramah he must have heard of the wonderful events which sometimes made the people of Israel tremble, sometimes filled them with joy and admiration; he must have heard of the miraculous power which had been given to the youthful Psalmist, to chase away the evil spirit which had taken possession of the mind of the king; he must have heard how the man of Gath had defied the armies of the living God, and how the good shepherd he had consecrated had gone forth in the *name* of the *Lord of Hosts*, and with *this* stone from the brook of living waters had bruised the head of the great adversary of his people. Samuel must also have heard how Saul, envious and jealous of the fame of his great deliverer, pursued the son of Jesse with implacable hatred and revenge. He must have heard, and trembled as he heard, of the cold-blooded ferocity which commanded the murder of the priests of the Temple, sparing neither women nor children, and burning their very city to the ground. Samuel must have heard all that the king had done, but neither zeal for God, nor fear for the sinner, nor compassion for the persecuted, induced the Prophet to seek again the presence of the king; he might, indeed, have looked upwards with an earnest desire, a passionate longing, that once more the voice of God might bid him arise and go forth to stem, if it were possible, those overflowings of ungodliness; but no voice was heard from Heaven, no ministry of mercy was committed again to the Prophet, and "Samuel came no more to see Saul until the day of his death." No more was that earnest voice heard in the palace at Gibeah, in accents of counsel, of warning, of encouragement in righteousness; the grave seemed already to have severed the king from the Prophet, and the dark curtain of eternity seemed to have been already drawn between the living and the dead. Very terrible is the thought, that the creature can so resolutely reject the word of God as to be finally left to himself; that he can so resist the Holy Ghost[1] as to have it said to him at last, "Be it unto thee even as thou wilt."

As the joyousness even of childhood is saddened by the silence on earth, when the merry bird droops its wing, and the busy hum of creation is hushed,

[1] Acts vii. 51.

in awful expectation of the coming storm, so the soul of the believer is oppressed at the silence in Heaven, when God has ceased to speak to the heart of the sinner, when the angel of mercy is arrested in his embassies of love, and forbidden any longer to minister to one who has thought scorn of his future inheritance, who has trampled upon the crown laid up for him in Heaven, who has wilfully ceased to be an heir of salvation.

But though Samuel came no more to see Saul till the day of his death, Saul found himself once more face to face with the Prophet of the Lord.

David, anointed as he had been by God king over Israel, was nevertheless at that time the very scorn of men, and the outcast of the people; hunted from place to place by the bloodhounds of Saul, he had fled at length to Ramah to unburden his mind to the Prophet, to tell him all that Saul had done against him, all that he had to endure from the hatred and jealousy of the king. The aged man, having listened to this sad recital of violence and cruelty, thinks it safer, on David's account, to remove from his home, and seek another dwelling at Naioth, though no fears for his personal safety had ever before made him flee from the face of Saul. The enemies of the king, however, are active in their search, and very quickly it was told to Saul that Samuel and David are at Naioth; messengers were accordingly sent to seize the son of Jesse, but when they approached to lay hold on their victim, "the spirit of God came upon them," and instead of doing the bidding of their master, they are compelled to speak the words which God puts into their mouth. Three times the messengers are miraculously prevented from accomplishing their purpose, and, like those who in after times were sent to seize a greater than David, they were obliged to go backward, and fall to the ground, overcome by an influence they were unable to resist. The king, with the boldness of a Judas, determined himself to attempt what his servants were unable to accomplish, but, instead of securing his prey, he is seized, like his messengers, with the spirit of prophecy, strips off his regal and military attire, and, shorn of all the trappings of worldly honour and dignity, lies (spell-bound) all night upon the earth before Samuel, in wonderful manifestation of the impotence of man and the power of God.

This is the last incident in the life of the Prophet recorded in Holy Scripture. The daring impiety of the king, and the sufferings of David must have cast a deep shade of sadness over the latter days of the man of God; he was, however, supported by that faith which is the substance of things hoped for, the evidence of things not seen, a faith which made him, like the other holy men of old, embrace the promises which he had seen afar off—confess that he was a stranger and pilgrim upon earth, and that he sought a better country, and a city that had foundations, that is a heavenly, which God had prepared for him[2]. Knowing that to die would to him be gain, joyfully must Samuel have welcomed the approach of that day which brought to his people the mournful tidings that the aged saint was no longer amongst them, that the Prophet had been taken to his everlasting rest. The heart of the nation was profoundly afflicted. Israel hastened to the dwelling-place of Samuel, to pay the last sad honours to the memory of the dead, and "a voice was heard in Ramah, lamentation and bitter weeping," the voice of a people weeping the loss of their friend and benefactor, and "refusing to be comforted because he was not."

The people mourned for Samuel. Was the bitter cry of the thousands of Israel heard in the palace of Gibeah? did it penetrate the heart of the proud and imperious monarch? Long and tenderly in the days of his flesh had "Samuel mourned for Saul." Did Saul now mourn for Samuel? Alas! how often does the death of those by whom we have been fondly loved fill with self-reproach the heart that deeply valued and sincerely returned their affection! how painfully, in the first moments of bereavement, does memory recall the past, and dwell upon trifling sorrows inflicted, small kindnesses neglected, inconsiderate words, not felt but hastily spoken, until grief magnifying these shortcomings makes the bereaved unjust to themselves, and ready to exclaim,

[2] See Heb. xi.

with the conscience-stricken brethren of Joseph, "We are verily guilty concerning our brother." If thoughts such as these can fill with bitterness the heart that has freely returned the love that was freely bestowed upon it, what must be the anguish of those who have repaid affection with indifference, and devotion with ingratitude? The death of the friend we have thus despised and rejected must surely be God's last appeal to the heart of the sinner, an appeal which must pierce that heart with sorrow and compunction, or render it hard and insensible for ever. How was this appeal received by the king? did it make him remember the days that were past, and the years that were gone by? did he call to mind the noble disinterestedness of the Prophet in willingly yielding up to him, as ruler of his people, the chief post in Israel? did he recall the day when Samuel had so loyally presented him to the assembled thousands at Mizpeh, and generously witnessed the enthusiasm with which they received the lord and governor they had chosen for themselves? did Saul think how Samuel had watched over him, counselled him, faithfully served, and honestly reproved him? and, then, did he think of the scorn, neglect, and persecution, with which he had brought the gray hairs of his aged friend and counsellor with sorrow to the grave? or did the king bid away these mournful and salutary thoughts, and resolutely quench perhaps the last dying spark of a generous mind and a kindly spirit? It is to be feared that this was the case; for nowhere do we hear that the monarch took part in the lamentations of his subjects; nowhere do we hear that Saul mourned for Samuel, or that any public tribute of respect was paid by him to the memory of the aged saint of the Lord. "The heart is desperately wicked, and deceitful above measure;" and so it may be that the king thought he had done well to be angry with the Prophet; that the old man, though meaning to be kind, had gone the wrong way with him, had irritated and threatened him, and set him against his duty, by continually reminding him of it. Nay, it may be feared that a feeling rather of joy, than of sorrow, might have taken possession of the mind of the king. For while Samuel lived he might ever have been in dread of some fresh declaration of God's anger, some merciful warning, to rouse him once again from his course of wilfulness and disobedience; but that dread was now at an end. The reprover's voice was silent in the grave, and the king was left to himself; at liberty to walk in a "light of his own making," and "to compass himself about with sparks of his own kindling;" at liberty to think "his own thoughts," and to follow his own ways; and so for a time the emancipated spirit might have rejoiced in the awful freedom with which God had made him free, to tread with unfettered steps the broad road which leadeth to destruction.

The history of Samuel is so indissolubly linked

in Holy Scripture with that of Saul, that it would have been impossible to pursue the one without considering the other; but death, which severs the closest of all earthly bonds, ought, it would seem, to have severed all future connexion between the Prophet and the king; and having followed, as we have done, the son of Hannah to his last resting-place the grave, having beheld him honourably buried, in his house at Ramah, amidst the tears and lamentations of the people of Israel, it would seem that nothing now remained but to meditate upon his virtues, and to profit by his example.

The history of this eminent saint of God does not however finish with his death; and to complete the record which Holy Scripture has given us of Samuel, it will be necessary for us briefly to follow to the end the fortunes of Saul, for once more the saint and the sinner must be brought together upon earth, once more the condemnation pronounced upon the king by the mouth of the living Prophet, must be confirmed by the voice of the risen Judge.

CHAPTER XIII.

SAUL SEEKS AFTER A WOMAN WITH A FAMILIAR SPIRIT.

THE death of Samuel prepared the way for the advent of David; the mantle of the Prophet was to fall upon the future king of Israel, and a double portion of his spirit was to rest upon the man after God's own heart. Saul's unceasing persecution of David showed that he was inwardly convinced of the truth of Samuel's repeated declarations, that the crown was to be plucked from his brow, and given to one worthier than himself. On two occasions the rare magnanimity of the son of Jesse drew an unequivocal declaration of this inward conviction from the king. In the cave of Engedi, when David cut off the skirts of the monarch's garment, in order to show him how easily he might have taken his life, Saul declared, "Behold, I know that thou shalt surely be king, and that the kingdom of Israel shall be established in thine hand;" and when, after the death of Samuel, in the wilderness of Ziph, David took the spear from the head of the king, and the cruse of water from his side,

and rousing up the sleeping guard reproached them
for carelessness and neglect of their master, Saul,
deeply affected, declared again his firm conviction
of the future greatness of his rival, saying, "Blessed
be thou, my son David: thou shalt both do great
things, and also thou shalt prevail." The heart of
Saul was, however, but as the flint, which violently
struck sends out the evanescent spark, and then
becomes as dark and as cold as ever; for very
quickly did the thoughts of hatred and revenge
resume their baneful influence over the mind of the
king, and his belief in the ultimate success and
elevation of David served only to increase his ani-
mosity, and intensify his determination wilfully to
struggle on to the last, and to fight against the
decree of his God. In such a conflict as this no
mortal has ever prevailed; the south wind may indeed for a time blow softly, and man in his presumption may suppose that he has gained his
purpose, but ere long an Euroclydon with fury
will arise to dissipate his vain and delusive expectations, and to shatter the frail vessel that was to
bear him in safety to the haven of his rest.

Four years had elapsed since the death of Samuel,
before the storm, which had been long preparing,
was suffered to burst with unmitigated violence
upon the devoted head of the king, and to lay in
the dust the proud and rebellious spirit which had
so long resisted the will of the Most High. Once
more the heathen are taken by God as "the rod of

His anger," and "the staff of His indignation[1]." "The Philistines gathered themselves together to fight against Israel, and came and pitched in Shunem, and Saul gathered all Israel together, and they pitched in Gilboa." It was nothing new or strange for Saul thus to find himself face to face with the constant and implacable enemy of his people. Why then was it, that "when he saw the host of the Philistines, he was afraid," and that "his heart greatly trembled?" What was it that, at this moment, made a coward of one of Israel's most distinguished warriors, of the man who had "his thousands slain," of the man who delighted in war, and whose ambition was continually craving to add more laurels to his crown? What was it that now made his heart tremble, and sink within him, at the sight of the foe he had so often met and vanquished? It was that foreboding of evil by which so many amongst the valiant sons of men have felt that their career of conquest was about to be ended, and their past glory tarnished by defeat.

Overcome with fear and perplexity, "Saul inquired of the Lord:" *how* he inquired, we know not, for he had made the house of God a desolation, and his hands were full of the blood of the priests of the Temple, of the blood of their innocent wives, of their helpless infants; still we are told that he inquired of the Lord. No answer, however, was vouchsafed to him either "by dream, or by Urim,

[1] Isa. x.

or by prophets." "I have called, and thou didst refuse to listen; I have stretched out My hand, but ye have set at nought all My counsel, and would none of My reproof: I also will laugh at your calamity; I will mock when your fear cometh; when your fear cometh as a desolation, and your destruction cometh as a whirlwind: when distress and anguish cometh upon you. Then shalt thou call upon Me, but I will not answer; thou shalt seek Me early, but thou shalt not find Me." The silence of the oracle seemed to convey no answer but this to the inquiry of the king. What then must Saul do? must he persevere in supplication, and watch unto prayer? must his eyes fail in looking upwards, and his heart faint in waiting upon his God? Alas! this was altogether impossible to one who had lived so long in habits of wilfulness and disobedience. Even now at the eleventh hour the proud spirit of the king refused to humble itself before God. According to the laws of the theocracy he had done what it was his duty to do; he *had* inquired of the Lord. The oracle had refused to answer him; God had abandoned him. What then? must he tamely and passively submit to this agonizing silence? must he remain in this state of miserable and restless uncertainty? No; it was better to be told the worst at once, than to live in the fear of it; an answer he *must* have, he *would* have; and if it could not be got from above, why, then he would seek it from below. Oh! how true were the words of Samuel, when he declared that "rebellion was as the sin of witchcraft, and stubbornness as iniquity and idolatry;" for the king, resolute in evil, determined at once to sever the last link which, outwardly at least, had till then bound him to the worship of Jehovah. With a boldness of purpose, and decision of character, which would have made him sublime, had it been found in the way of righteousness, he commissioned his servants to seek him out a woman with a familiar spirit, that he might inquire of her, that he might, from the incantations of the necromancer, obtain the knowledge which had been denied him by the oracle of God.

Here, however, his past faithfulness seemed to rise up in pity, and to present an insurmountable obstacle to the dark and desperate purpose of his soul.

In his earlier days, when God's word was a "lamp to his feet, and a light to his paths," the king had been very zealous in putting wizards and all who had familiar spirits out of the land; for the mixed multitude who had followed the exodus from Egypt had been like the remnant of the Canaanites, "pricks in the eyes of the Israelites, and thorns in their sides," by keeping alive in their minds the abominable idolatries of that land of intellectual light and spiritual darkness; and very terrible was the power which the arts of the sorcerer exercised in exciting the imagination, and in corrupting the weak, wayward, and unstable minds of God's ancient people. It was therefore expedient that measures severe in the extreme should be taken against all those who sought to draw them away from the worship of the one true God.

It is not quite certain that the punishment of death was awarded to every species of divination, to those, for instance, who simply employed fascinations and drew presages and omens from natural things without prejudice to others; but it is quite certain that the law was imperative against those whom, it is said, Saul had put out of the land, against the " sorcerer, wizard, and all who had familiar spirits;" for those wretched creatures, those base deceivers of their brethren (themselves, it may be, also deceived by the arch-enemy of souls [a]), pretended, like the spiritualists of our own day, to the possession of wonderful and superhuman powers. Through the mysterious agency of what they called their "Familiar," they professed to lift the veil which severs the world of spirits from the world of sense, to unlock the prison-house of the grave, and to compel the

---

[a] "It has been held, that when the systems of ancient idolatry offered to the Evil One convenient and prepared agencies through which he might operate, he did so operate, using the deluded wretches who sought for powers beyond nature as his tools for riveting the chains which, during many long ages, held the human mind bound in darkness and degradation. There is much in Scripture to sanction this conclusion." See Kitto on Deut. xviii. 10.

departed to return to the earth, and hold converse again with the living, and to read for them the dread secrets of the future, which "lie hid in the folds of the divine predestination;" they thus "inquired for the living to the dead[a];" these iniquitous usurpers of the divine prerogative "hunted the souls of God's people," "strengthened the hands of the wicked that they should not return from their wicked way, by promising them life," and "made the hearts of the righteous sad, whom God had not made sad," by their lying divinations; cunning, crafty, and thoroughly versed in the weaknesses of human nature, they practised upon the living soul, as the cruel experimental anatomist practises upon the living subject. When it suited their purpose they could touch the tenderest and most susceptible nerve, and make it tremble and quiver in anguish, whilst they looked on unmoved, doubtless often secretly rejoicing at the torment their art was inflicting. Well would it have been for Saul, had he indeed succeeded in altogether ridding the land of these abominable superstitions; unfortunately, however, the evil though suppressed had not been eradicated, and as it is the melancholy privilege of the great to have about them obsequious and unprincipled followers, only too ready to do their bidding, the commission of Saul was speedily executed, for by

---

[a] Necromancer literally means "one that seeks to or inquires of the dead."

diligent search a woman with a familiar spirit is found still secretly carrying on her iniquitous traffic in making merchandise of men's souls. But here an obstacle again presented itself to the safe accomplishment of the desire of the king; the dwelling-place of this woman was at Endor, and to reach it was at that moment an undertaking full of difficulty and danger, for the Philistines had gathered together all their armies to Aphek, a village which still exists on the slope of the range of hills called Little Hermon. On the opposite side, on the rise of Mount Gilboa, hard by the spring of Jezreel, was the army of Saul. The village of Endor [4] was situated immediately facing Mount Tabor, on the other side of the range of Little Hermon, so that in order to get to the abode of the necromancer it was actually necessary for Saul to cross the shoulder of the ridge on which the Philistines were encamped. The heart of the king, however, had not shrunk from the sin of the undertaking, neither would it shrink from the peril which it involved; his mind was irrevocably made up to risk the consequence of his rashness and the anger of his God.

This sad page in the history of the carnal mind's rebellion against its Maker very forcibly proves that "if there be first the willing mind," it is in truth

---

[4] "Large caves which, at least to modern notions, accord with the residence of the necromancer, still perforate the rocky sides of the hill."—See Stanley's beautiful chapter, "The Plain of Esdraelon," "Sinai and Palestine," p. 337.

far easier for man to work out his own salvation than to work out his own destruction; for as He that is with us is greater than he that is against us, so one-half the painful effort made by Saul to stifle the voice of conscience, one-half the energy, perseverance, and determination put forth to carry out his sinful purpose, in spite of every discouragement, of every obstacle, so mercifully thrown in his way, would have enabled him successfully to fight against the power of temptation, to break loose from the snares of the Evil One, to win the precious boon of the Divine forgiveness, and to place himself once more under the shadow of the Almighty, and within the magic circle of the Everlasting Arms.

CHAPTER XIV.

THE RAISING OF SAMUEL AT ENDOR.

It was night in the camp at Gilboa, where the hosts of Israel had been gathered together in anticipation of the conflict which awaited them. A welcome pause had succeeded to the din and turmoil of the day—

"Sleep, Nature's soft nurse,"

had drawn her quiet mantle around many a young and enthusiastic bosom, whilst the more devout and thoughtful amongst the people, unwilling to lose in forgetfulness the last hours, perhaps, given them for preparation, watched unto prayer, prayed for themselves and for those who were sleeping around them, for those who might, before the night of tomorrow, sleep the sleep which knows no waking upon earth. Doubtless, the righteous prayed also for their king, prayed that God would preserve him from the shafts of the enemy, would give him a spirit of discretion and valour in the day of battle, and a spirit of humility and piety in the hour of victory. Little did they think that he for whom they prayed had deserted his post, and left them to themselves; little did they think that, putting off the outward garb of royalty, and the inward dignity of his high position, he had disguised himself as best he could, and, accompanied by two of his attendants, had, on this eventful night, left his state without a head and his camp without a leader. Little, too, did the Philistine dream that a prize so valuable as the person of the king of Israel was almost within his grasp; little could either friend or foe have believed that one who had so often been privileged to drink of the

> "Brook that flowed
> Hard by the oracle of God,"

could have thus forsaken the fountain of living waters [1], to hew for himself a broken cistern, which could hold no water, by seeking light from the power of darkness, and truth from "the father of lies." Saul was no ignorant idolater; he had never bowed the knee to the stock and the stone, saying, "Deliver me, for thou art my god;" he had never "bid the dumb wood awake, saying, It shall teach us." The infidel doctrines of the Sadducee, who believed in neither angel nor spirit, the deluding theories of the disputer of this world, who solves the difficulties of revelation by substituting in their stead still greater difficulties of his own imagining, were unknown in those earlier ages of the history of Israel. The record of creation had been too

[1] Jer. ii. 13.

recently given, and the people "had heard with their ears, and their fathers had told them" too much of "the noble works which God had done in their days, and in the old time before them," to question the miracles of Omnipotence, or to receive the Pentateuch as a castigated mythology. Saul believed in the Almighty Creator of heaven and earth; he believed in Him "who made the stars also," those stars which were lighting him on his way to destruction, impotent alike to impede or to impel the destinies of man. Saul believed both in angel and spirit; he believed in a life beyond the grave, otherwise he would not now be seeking "for the living to the dead[2]." Saul had belief, but he had not faith; for while belief may be merely the assent of the reason to facts which the senses, or the understanding, are obliged to admit, *faith* must be the *subjection* of the heart to truths which are "spiritually discerned;" and while faith (so long as it lives) *must* fight against sin, and if overcome for a time, *must* rise again, and conquer at last, *mere* belief may passively exist, with unrestrained rebellion against the power it has not ceased to acknowledge, and a determination to provoke the wrath which it has not ceased to fear. Thus was it with Saul; he closed his ears to the truth he believed, he shut his eyes to the judgment he dreaded; he would not listen to the words behind him, saying,

[2] Isa. viii. 19.

"Return unto Me, and I will return unto you;" he refused to look back, though to look back might have been his salvation. Strengthening himself, it may be, with the delusive idea that the object he had in view might justify the unhallowed means he was taking to compass it, with rapid footsteps he hurried on to his ruin, and never halted until he reached the abode of the necromancer, and stood in the presence of the woman whom, in other days, he would have swept from the face of the earth, as the base seducer and deceiver of his people.

With all her art the Witch of Endor is unable to see through the disguise of the king, but his majestic height and noble bearing, which could not be entirely concealed, added to the presence of his attendants, seem to have impressed her at once with the conviction that the mysterious visitor was no common individual. She is therefore alarmed, and unwilling, at first, to commit herself by exercising her art at the bidding of one who might possibly betray her. "And the woman said unto him, Behold, thou knowest what Saul hath done, how he hath cut off those that have familiar spirits, and the wizards, out of the land; wherefore then layest thou a snare for my life, to cause me to die[a]?" To quiet her apprehensions, the king swore to her by the Lord, whose laws he was transgressing, that no punishment should happen to her. "As the Lord liveth, said

---

[a] 1 Sam. xxviii. 9.

the king, there shall no punishment happen to thee for this thing." Wonderful power of the name of the Lord, even in this den of iniquity! Saul uses it to enforce the truth of his declaration, and the woman accepts it as a pledge of the stranger's fidelity. Her suspicions laid aside, she prepares herself to yield to the wishes of the stranger; before, however, she begins her incantations, it is necessary she should know whose spirit she is to summon from the dead.

The king had reigned for forty years, so that some of his favourites must have died in his service. Whom amongst them was the woman to bring up? Was it the beloved wife of his bosom, whose loss, for a time, had made the world a desolation? Was it the flattering courtier, ever ready to speak smooth things, to prophesy deceits, and to say to the troubled conscience, "Peace, peace, when there was no peace?" Was it the able warrior, whose valour had cost him his life, and whose counsels might prove a tower of strength against the approaching attack of the enemy?

No, it was none of these that Saul would now summon from the grave; it was the upright counsellor, the stern reprover, the true-hearted minister of God. It was upon Samuel the king leant in this hour of tribulation, it was to see Samuel again, it was for this alone that Saul had taken the perilous journey to Endor. Trusting to a love which he believed had outlived the grave, to a tenderness which death could not annihilate, he imagined that if only he could see Samuel again, if only he could tell him of his deep distress, of his agonizing perplexity, all might yet be well; there might still for him be hope, there might still for him be salvation. Oh! surely, surely, as in life, so in death was Samuel a wondrous type of Him, the last stay of the desolate, the last refuge of the sinner.

To the question of the woman, "Whom shall I bring up unto thee?" Saul unhesitatingly replies, "Bring me up Samuel," and no sooner have the words escaped from his lips than the Prophet appears, not at the bidding of the woman, not through the art of the necromancer, but at the call of the king, and by the permission of the Most High. It is now her turn to be affrighted, who had hitherto played upon the feelings of others. The names of Samuel and Saul must have been inseparably associated in the mind of the woman, and the mention of the one enabled her at once to detect the presence of the other, and, terrified by the supernatural appearance of the Prophet, she exclaims, "Why hast thou deceived me? for thou art Saul!"

Not daring himself to look upon the apparition, Saul said unto her, "Be not afraid: for what seest thou? And the woman said unto Saul, I saw gods ascending out of the earth." From this description we are given to understand that the Prophet brought with him from the abode of the blessed some dazzling radiance, like that which accompanied the rising of Moses and Elias at the transfiguration of our Lord; the woman must have known that the Elohim, the Great Jehovah of the Jews, "the Lord their God," had been wont to manifest Himself to His people by the Shekinah, a cloud " of excellent glory," so it was very natural for her, seeing this luminous appearance, to infer from it the presence of God Himself, or of one who was sent to represent Him. Saul, still fearing to look upon the risen Prophet, seeks a description of his person, and said unto the woman, " What form is he of?" And she said, "An old man cometh up, and he is covered with a mantle." The king is no longer in doubt as to who it is that the woman is looking upon, he knows that it is Samuel; he sees him as he last beheld him, his venerable form bent with age, and worn out with grief and disappointment. The mention of that sacerdotal robe, always worn by the Prophet, must also have vividly recalled to the mind of the king that last fatal day on which, having laid hold on that mantle, it was rent from his eager grasp, and the rending made a symbol of his own future rejection from being king over Israel. Overcome by an internal conviction of the reality of the awful presence of the man of God, full of reverence and fear, the proud spirit, which had so often rebelled against the living Mediator, quailed at once before the risen Judge; "for Saul stooped with his face to the ground, and bowed himself." "And Samuel said unto Saul, Why hast thou disquieted me, to bring me up?" Had the shadow of a doubt remained upon the mind of the king as to its being really the Prophet, these few words of awful solemnity, of reproachful tenderness, would have convinced him that no one but Samuel could have uttered them. Why hast thou disquieted me? Was it not enough, he would seem to say, that while living thou didst grieve me continually with thy sins, and persecute me with thine enmity, but that even in death thou must break the repose of the grave, and draw down the spirit from on high, once more to witness thy despair, once more to grieve over thy fall, once more to reiterate thy condemnation? Why hast thou disquieted me to bring me up? Alas! what can the wretched monarch do, when thus solemnly interrogated, but cast his sin upon God, and plead as his excuse the inexorable silence of the Almighty? "And Saul answered, I am sore distressed; for the Philistines make war against me, and God is departed from me, and answereth me no more, neither by prophets, nor by dreams: therefore I have called thee, that thou mayest make known unto me what I shall do." As God did not, would not answer him, *therefore* he has forced himself to seek "for the living to the dead." With the remarkable simplicity, the straightforward truthfulness, so characteristic of the living Samuel, the Prophet at once dismisses the irreverent plea of the conscience-stricken monarch. Then said Samuel, "Wherefore then dost thou ask of me, seeing the Lord is departed from thee, and is become thine enemy? and the Lord hath done to him, as He spake by me: for the Lord hath rent the kingdom out of thine hand, and given it to thy neighbour, even to David." "Moreover the Lord will also deliver Israel with thee into the hand of the Philistines: and to-morrow shalt thou and thy sons be with me: the Lord also shall deliver the host of Israel into the hand of the Philistines." Yes, infatuated and miserable sinner! the knowledge thou didst so ardently crave after, was but the knowledge of thine own approaching and inevitable destruction; "for as the fire devoureth the stubble, and the flame consumeth the chaff, so thy root shall be as rottenness, and thy blossoms shall go up as the dust, because thou hast cast away the law of the Lord, and despised the word of the Holy One of Israel." Lo! to-morrow must thou and thy sons prepare to lie down with the Prophet in the grave. Where then shall be the things for which thou hast bartered thine everlasting inheritance, which thou hast given in exchange for thy soul? They shall all evade thine eager grasp. The kingdom thou didst glory in shall pass away to another. The warlike host, the arm of flesh, in which thou didst put thy trust, shall be scattered. Thy goodly sons who were to perpetuate thy dynasty, even Jonathan, the good and the brave, all must go down with thee, there, "where the wicked cease from troubling, and the weary are at rest;" there, where the saint and the sinner, the persecuted and the persecutor, the vanquished and the victor, are at peace together; for there ambition has no voice, and glory no charm; there, "the sound of the viol has ceased," the pomp of the mighty is at an end; he that was a terror in the land of the living is silent in darkness, and his sword is laid under his head[4]; for he has no other pillow in his last resting-place,— the grave.

In this great mausoleum, this house of many mansions, must thou and thy sons be with the Prophet to-morrow.

Oh, fearful announcement! inexorable decree! How full of horror to one so little prepared to receive it! No wonder the unhappy monarch, with a mind harassed by fear and anxiety, and a body faint, fasting, and exhausted with fatigue, should have sunk insensible to the earth, should have become unconscious for a time of the terrible fate which awaited him.

[4] See Ezek. xxxii. 27.

CHAPTER XV.

BATTLE OF MOUNT GILBOA.

The besetting sin of the first king of Israel in the latter years of his reign, was a lawlessness of spirit, a reckless determination "to do according to his own will," which made him utterly regardless of the consequences of his actions. In going to consult the witch of Endor, no one knew better than he did the heinous nature of the sin he was committing, the extent of the danger he incurred, and the ruin and humiliation it would bring upon himself and upon his people, if by accident or treachery he fell into the hand of the enemy. Yet he persevered, for concealed under the disguise he had assumed, and favoured by the shadows of the night, he fancied himself secure from every eye but the eye of the friends who attended him. Perhaps he might have paused before he so fearfully committed himself, had he for a moment imagined that what he was thus doing secretly would one day be proclaimed openly, had he thought that not only his shame and degradation would be revealed in the page of Inspired History to Israel his people, but that his name would go down to posterity, for ever associated with the infamous name of the necromantic woman. Saul had once declared of himself, " I have played the fool exceedingly;" and in "seeking for the living to the dead," again might he most truly have repeated this humiliating confession: for he had deluded himself with the fond imagination, that though the Creator had forsaken him, the creature might help him; he had vainly expected that Samuel might bring with him from the world of spirits some favourable interpretation of the silence of the oracle, some new revelation of the purposes of the Deity, some cheering assurance that the judgment which God had threatened He had never intended to execute. Samuel was permitted to appear; the risen Prophet, however, came but to reiterate the word which had been spoken before by the living minister of God. Twice at Gilgal the very same condemnation had been pronounced against the king, and nothing now was added to what he already knew, but an intimation of the defeat of his army, and the speedy execution of the sentence against himself and his posterity, which, in mercy, had been so long delayed. The same condemnation, however, which before had been listened to with indifference, came now with the overwhelming and realizing power of truth upon the soul. All vain expectations, all unsubstantial theories, were overthrown for ever. Saul now felt that to reason against God's word would be useless, to cavil at it unavailing, and to set it aside impossible; the stout heart of the natural man, the intellectual power of the ruler, and the courage of the warrior, all gave way at once, and he who had so often been lovingly *entreated*, was now sternly *compelled* to yield himself to God.

Thus will it be with every one of us hereafter. The unprofitable servant, who, despising the grace given him, buried his master's gift in the depths of an earthly, perverse, and cavilling spirit, will be tried by no impressions or opinions of his own, by no new revelation from above; the word which he had heard and rejected, "the same shall judge him at the last day [1]."

This last day had, however, not yet come for Israel's sinful monarch; to this last awful and final account he had not yet been summoned; for, raised from the ground by the care of his attendants, he once more opened his eyes to the light of this world, once more consciousness returned, and with it the remembrance of the past; and although, as he gazed around him, all trace of the supernatural appearance had vanished, yet the words which the Prophet had uttered were written in letters of fire upon the brain of the king. He knew that he had been deposed from his kingdom, and that his majesty, glory, and honour had been taken from him, and given to another. Why then should he seek to prolong so miserable an existence? Impetuous and self-willed even in his despair, he determined to refuse all

---

[1] John xii. 48.

bodily sustenance, and thus to anticipate his doom. A ray of God's light seems at this moment to pierce through the gloom which surrounds this dark abode of sin and of sorrow. The witch of Endor, the wretched being whose life had hitherto been spent in the service of Satan, instead of rejoicing at the fall of her bitterest enemy, instead of exulting over the humiliation of the persecutor of herself and her people, comes forward to help and to comfort him. Generously she devotes to his service all that she has to offer; with ready hand she prepares the one poor calf, which, it is said[2], was all her living; and her voice, the persuasive voice of genuine sympathy and respectful tenderness, joined to the urgent entreaties of his attendants, at length succeeds in inducing the king to abandon his suicidal determination, and to sit up and eat of the meat which is set before him. Strengthened by the food thus hospitably prepared, soothed, it may be, by meeting with a feeling of kindliness where he might reasonably have expected a spirit of retaliation, Saul is enabled once more to resume his disguise, and to retrace his steps to the heights of Gilboa, and on leaving the dwelling of the sorceress, may we not hope that he left behind him one, who, awfully impressed with the manifestation of the power of Jehovah, would from henceforth burn her books, abjure her evil arts, and turn from darkness unto light, from sin unto righteousness?

[2] See Josephus.

There is no respect of persons with God; the immortal soul of the peasant is as precious in His sight as the soul of the monarch; and so it is recorded of the Saviour, that on one memorable occasion when He trod as man the wilderness of this world, though wearied and faint with the journey of the day, He nevertheless "must needs go through Samaria," because in that despised locality a poor creature would be found willing to listen to His word, and to receive for the cleansing of her soul, that "living water" of which whosoever drinketh shall "never thirst again." May we not, therefore, be permitted to hope, that like the woman of Samaria, the woman of Endor was snatched as a brand from the burning, by that gracious Being, who, under the old as well as under the new dispensation, has ever proclaimed Himself as "the Lord, the Lord God, merciful and gracious, longsuffering and abundant in goodness and truth?"

If the words which the Prophet had spoken, though a savour of death unto death to the king, were by the mercy of God made a savour of life unto life to the woman, Samuel had not been disquieted in vain. But while thus hoping the best for the one poor sinner, are we compelled to fear the worst for the other? Must we indeed believe that for Saul no place was found for repentance? The sentence pronounced by the Prophet against the king was limited entirely to the perishing things of this world, the defeat of his army, the destruction of his dynasty, and the life of the body ; no judgment was pronounced upon the future destiny of the immortal spirit, for there is no instance in the Old Testament, and only one [a] in the New, in which God has anticipated his final judgment on the soul of the sinner.

Are we therefore justified from the silence of the Prophet in believing that as to-morrow the earthly remains of the king would be with Samuel in the grave, so to-morrow his immortal spirit would be with him in paradise? May we rest in the cheering conviction that Saul, effectually converted by having been the subject of so stupendous a miracle, by having heard the voice of one who had risen from the dead, believed at last unto righteousness, brought at last the sacrifice of a broken and a contrite spirit, so that his sins, " red as scarlet, were made white as snow," through the atoning efficacy of the blood of the Lamb slain from the foundation of the world? Alas! the subsequent history of the unfortunate monarch gives no encouragement to

[a] "It is with awe we behold in Judas the only one who received his sentence in person before the last day."—Ellicott, Hulsean Lectures.

Our truly Scriptural Church has well remembered this, for in committing earth to earth, ashes to ashes, dust to dust, in sure and certain hope of the resurrection to eternal life through our Lord Jesus Christ, she leaves in all reverence and humility the soul of the sinner to the judgment of her God.

the belief that the little moment which intervened between his return to the camp and the battle of Mount Gilboa was spent by the sinner in penitence and in supplication. Had David been there, such might have been the case; once again the fervent piety of the son of Jesse might have cast out the evil spirit and roused into life the better feelings of the king. Once again the fever of his soul might have been refreshed by the sweet voice of the Psalmist, as the panting hart is refreshed by the sound of the water-brooks, as the burning brow is refreshed by the health-inspiring breeze. But David was not there; an exile from the house of his father, he had been compelled to seek refuge in an alien's country, and to crave a home from the hospitality of the stranger: and in thus banishing David, the ill-fated monarch had banished the good physician of his soul, and rudely thrust aside the tender hand that might have healed him; and not only had Saul severed the tie of love and gratitude, which should have bound him to his benefactor, but he must also have isolated himself from the affectionate and confidential intercourse of the pious Jonathan, and of the good and the wise among his people. What then remained but that he should turn for support and consolation to those unrighteous followers who had helped him on to his ruin? And what could be expected of earthly-minded and unprincipled advisers, but that they should seek even to the last, by the incense of flattery, and the sophistries of unbelief, to draw away the mind of the king from the fears which oppressed him? Perhaps they might have tried to induce their royal master to doubt the reality of the scene which he had witnessed at Endor. The contradictions involved in the words of the apparition, and the impossibility of these words being realized, might have been urged as an all-sufficient reason for rejecting the prophecy, and for considering it but as a lying divination unworthy of exciting a moment's apprehension in the mind of the king.

And most assuredly it was very difficult to believe that Israel could be at once both humbled and exalted, vanquished and victorious; it required very great dependence on God's Omnipotence to believe that the triumph of the Philistine could lead to the elevation of David, for the Philistine was fighting not to give another king to Israel, but to overturn the monarchy, and to enslave or annihilate the people. It certainly did seem incredible, that an enemy who had overcome the well-trained armies of Saul, should himself be overcome by David[4], and that one who had been set aside and neglected by his own people should be able in a moment to pluck the crown from the brow of the illustrious monarch who had made Israel the terror of the heathen, and the first among the nations of the earth.

This prophecy of the risen Samuel did indeed seem past belief, for it must be remembered that at the

[4] 1 Sam. xxix 4

time it was uttered Saul was even more powerful than when he had "fought against Moab, and the children of Ammon, and Edom, and the kings of Zobah," than when he had "vexed his enemies on every side," than when he had vanquished these very Philistines, now gathered together against him; for as it has been before observed, in the short intervals of peace the efforts of the king had been unremitting in adding to the numbers and strength of his army, thus increasing continually its power and its efficiency. Abner, the experienced chieftain, the prudent, skilful, and successful leader of a thousand fights, was still the captain of the hosts of Israel. The valiant Jonathan, who, with his little band of twenty men, had once smitten the garrison of the enemy, and made the very earth to tremble at his presence, was preparing once more to conquer or to die in the service of his country, and Abinadab and Melchi-shua were also ready to lay down their lives in defence of their rightful inheritance: what then was wanting to ensure the success of the king, and make the victory his own?

Nothing, it may be answered, absolutely nothing was wanting to Saul, but that without which human strength is weakness, and human skill of no avail,—the blessing of the Almighty.

The all-important to-morrow which was to determine the truth or the falsehood of the prophecy of Samuel, came at last, and with it the deadly conflict. The king once more in the presence of his people, and surrounded by a noble band of loyal and devoted followers, was "himself again," forgetting, it may be, in the excitement of the moment, the words heard at Endor, and while bravely leading on his troops against the enemy, hoping perhaps once more to lead them on to glory and to victory. But, alas! though man may forget, God remembers, for "heaven and earth may pass away," but His word can never pass away "until all be fulfilled." And thus was it seen that day on the plain of Esdraelon; for Abner was discomfited, and Israel fled before the Philistines, and Jonathan was cut down, like a beauteous ear of corn which the sun has delighted to ripen; and Abinadab and Melchi-shua lay dead upon the battle-field, and the king in despair, rushing into the thick of the fight, seeking death, but not finding it, wrested the fatal shaft from the hand of Omnipotence, and died as he had lived, a rebel to the law of his God.

Thus the mighty had fallen, and the weapons of war had perished, and the shield of Saul had been vilely cast away, as if he had not been anointed with oil, "and the hearts of the men of Israel," on the other side of the valley, "and on the other side of the Jordan," failing them for fear, they abandoned their cities, and fled for their lives. The triumph of the Philistine, however, was but for a moment; for as in the day that the man of Gath defied the armies of the living God, the son of Jesse was sent to crush the power of the adversary; so now, a second time, he appears for the salvation of his people, and the destruction of their oppressors. At his first coming, the deliverance he had wrought for Israel had been rewarded with ingratitude, ignominy, and persecution. At his second coming all was changed: invested with power and authority, and guided by the word of the Lord, he went up to Hebron, and took possession of the cities of Judah; for as the promise of everlasting dominion was given to Judah, the men of Judah were the first to receive the anointed of the Lord, to acknowledge his supremacy, and to choose him for their king.

The words which Samuel had spoken when alive had never been suffered to fall to the ground; so the words which he had spoken from the grave had in like manner been marvellously fulfilled; for the man of the earth had been laid low, and his sons had been numbered with the dead, and the hosts of Israel had been given into the power of the Philistine; and though separated for a time from their brethren of Judah, Israel and Judah became one again in the hand of the Lord; for after a reign of seven years in Hebron as king of the Jews, the supremacy of the son of Jesse was recognized by all the other tribes of Israel, and the man after God's own heart was privileged to reunite the dispersed of his people, to bring them back again into one fold and under one shepherd, to feed them with a faithful and true heart, and to rule them prudently with all his power.

Thus Samuel, beloved of his Lord, "*established a kingdom*," and by his faithfulness was found a true Prophet.

CHAPTER XVI.

CONCLUSION.

WHEN the Lord Jesus bowed the heavens and came down to visit us, He took upon Himself the threefold office of our Priest, our Prophet, and our King. As Priest He was prefigured by Melchisedek, as King by David, and as Prophet by Samuel; for Samuel among the prophets stands pre-eminently distinguished as a type of our Lord. The beautiful simplicity and unadorned truthfulness of the teaching of the son of Hannah, his righteous severity against sin, joined to his loving tenderness for the sinner, his zeal and devotion, his patriotism and his loyalty, his readiness to humble himself, and at the bidding of his Heavenly Father to become as a servant to those over whom he had once ruled as a master, are traits of light in the character of the Prophet, which, like the faint streaks of the morning, shadow forth the brightness of the meridian sun.

It has been already observed that Samuel was the only saint of the Lord called when a child to the dignity of the prophetical office, and in the Scripture record of his apparition to the king of Israel we have the first ghost story ever given to the world, understanding, as we do, by a ghost story the sudden mysterious return, and the as sudden mysterious disappearance of one we have known and lived with on earth: and not only is the raising of Samuel the first ghost story on record, but it is the only one to be found in the pages of Holy Writ; and it is very remarkable that from Genesis to the Apocalypse, the only words recorded as having been spoken from the dead to the living, are the words spoken by Samuel to Saul, by the risen Prophet to the apostate king.

In the Old Testament and in the New, when the dead have been raised, it was to retake their mortal bodies, and to recommence their mortal life upon earth. When Moses and Elias were seen in glory on the Mount of the Transfiguration, though we know the subject of their discourse, the words spoken by them were never recorded, nor had they ever lived in personal intercourse with the three favoured Apostles, who could only have known them by a revelation from above. When the bodies of the Old Testament saints rose at the crucifixion of our Lord, nowhere are we told what they uttered, nor have we any reason to believe that under the Gospel dispensation the departed spirit of apostle, saint, or martyr, was ever sent back to the world, to encourage the faithful, or to rebuke the wicked. And when we consider that a return of the spirits from the dead was held alike by the Heathen, the Pagan,

L

and the Jew; when we consider that all pretended revelations given to the world, including the Koran, the Talmud, and the traditions of the Romish Church, are filled with apparitions and communications from the world of spirits, this one exception found in the whole history of the Bible must be received as a proof that the "land beyond this sable shore" is indeed a "bourne from which no traveller returns;" that though the living will go to the dead, the dead can never, except by the miraculous intervention of the Deity, come back to the living, the pious dead having reached a haven of rest where no sorrow can follow them, and where they can never again, like Samuel, be disquieted by the folly and the wickedness of those they have left behind them upon earth; and if in this case as in others it can be truly said that the exception proves the rule, may it not also be said that the rule proves the exception? for if God so continually watched over the truthfulness of His word, if He so guarded its genuineness as for the space of upwards of three thousand years never to permit any spurious or fictitious embodying of prevailing superstitions or spiritual delusions to creep into its pages, and to destroy its veracity, must we not then believe this *one* exception to have been a miraculous departure from the general laws of His kingdom, brought about by His own unfettered and sovereign will?

In their primary and literal meaning the words spoken by the risen Prophet at Endor have been fulfilled in the history of the past; in their higher and typical signification they will have another and a more stupendous accomplishment in the history of the future, when our "Lord Jesus Christ, whom the Heaven must receive until the times of restitution of all things," shall be sent once more " to accomplish what God hath spoken by the mouth of all His holy Prophets since the world began," for "that was not first which is spiritual, but that which is natural, and afterwards that which is spiritual;" for the first *David* is "of the earth, earthy," the second *David* " is the Lord from Heaven."

THE END.

LONDON:
GILBERT AND RIVINGTON, PRINTERS,
ST. JOHN'S SQUARE.

October, 1863.

A

SELECT LIST OF WORKS

PUBLISHED BY

MESSRS. RIVINGTON,

3, WATERLOO PLACE, PALL MALL, LONDON;

AND 41, HIGH STREET, OXFORD.

Adams's (Rev. W.) The Shadow of the Cross; an Allegory.
A New Edition, elegantly printed in crown 8vo., with Illustrations.
3s. 6d. *in extra cloth, gilt edges.*

—— The Shadow of the Cross; an Allegory.

—— The Distant Hills; an Allegory.

—— The Old Man's Home; an Allegorical Tale.

—— The King's Messengers; an Allegory.
New Editions of the above are now ready, in 18mo., with Engravings,
price 9d. *each in paper covers, or* 1s. *in limp cloth.*

—— A Collected Edition of the Four Allegories, with
Memoir and Portrait of the Author: elegantly printed in crown 8vo. 9s.
in cloth, or 14s. *in morocco.*

—— An Illustrated Edition of the above Sacred Allegories, with numerous Engravings on Wood from Original Designs by
C. W. Cope, R.A., J. C. Horsley, A.R.A., Samuel Palmer, Birket
Foster, and George E. Hicks. Small 4to. 21s. *in extra cloth; or* 36s. *in antique morocco.*

—— The Warnings of the Holy Week; being a Course
of Parochial Lectures for the Week before Easter, and the Easter Festivals.
Fifth Edition. Small 8vo. 4s. 6d.

Alford's (Dean) Greek Testament; with a critically revised Text: a Digest of Various Readings: Marginal References to Verbal and Idiomatic Usage: Prolegomena: and a copious Critical and Exegetical Commentary in English. In 4 vols. 8vo. 5*l.* 2*s.*

Or, separately,
Vol. I.—The Four Gospels. Fifth Edition. 28*s.*
Vol. II.—Acts to II. Corinthians. Fourth Edition. 24*s.*
Vol. III.—Galatians to Philemon. Third Edition. 18*s.*
Vol. IV.—Hebrews to Revelation. Second Edition. 32*s.*
The Fourth Volume may still be had in Two Parts.

———— **New Testament for English Readers**: containing the Authorized Version, with Marginal Corrections of Readings and Renderings; Marginal References; and a Critical and Explanatory Commentary. In Two large Volumes, 8vo.
Vol. I., Part I., containing the first three Gospels, with a Map of the Journeyings of our Lord, is now ready, price 12*s.*

———— **Sermons on Christian Doctrine**, preached in Canterbury Cathedral, on the Afternoons of the Sundays in the year 1861-62. Second Edition. Crown 8vo. 7*s.* 6*d.*

———— **Sermons preached at Quebec Chapel, 1854 to 1857.** In Seven Volumes, small 8vo. 2*l.* 1*s.*

Sold separately as follows:—
Vols. I. and II. (A course for the Year.) Second Edition. 12*s.* 6*d.*
Vol. III. (On Practical Subjects.) 7*s.* 6*d.*
Vol. IV. (On Divine Love.) Third Edition. 5*s.*
Vol. V. (On Christian Practice.) Second Edition. 5*s.*
Vol. VI. (On the Person and Office of Christ.) 5*s.*
Vol. VII. (Concluding Series.) 6*s.*

———— **Homilies on the Former Part of the Acts of the Apostles** (Chap. I.—X.); delivered at Quebec Chapel. 8vo. 8*s.*

———— **Poetical Works.** Third Edition. Crown 8vo. 8*s.* 6*d.*

American Church.—Recent Recollections of the Anglo-American Church in the United States. By an English Layman, five years resident in that Republic. 2 vols. post 8vo. 18*s.*

Anderson's (Hon. Mrs.) Practical Religion exemplified, by Letters and Passages from the Life of the late Rev. Robert Anderson, of Brighton. Sixth Edition. Small 8vo. 4*s.*

Anderson's (Rev. J. S. M.) Addresses, chiefly to Young Men. *Contents:*—1. On the Profitable Employment of Hours gained from Business. 2. Dr. Johnson. 3. Columbus. 4. Sir Walter Raleigh. 5. England and her Colonies. Second Edition. Small 8vo. 4*s.* 6*d.*

Annual Register; or, a View of the Political History and Domestic Occurrences of each year; published annually, price 18*s.*

Arnold's (Rev. T. K.) School-books (see page 18).

Arnold's (Rev. T. K.) Sermons preached in a Country Village. Post 8vo. 5s. 6d.

Arnold's (Rev. Dr. T.) History of Rome, from the Earliest Period to the End of the Second Punic War. New Edition. 3 vols. 8vo. 36s.

―――――――――――― History of the later Roman Commonwealth, from the End of the Second Punic War to the Death of Julius Cæsar, with the Reign of Augustus, and a Life of Trajan. New Edition. 2 vols. 8vo. 24s.

Aspinall's (Rev. James) Parish Sermons, as preached from his own Pulpit. In 2 vols. small 8vo. 5s. each.

Atkins's (Rev. Dr.) Six Discourses on Pastoral Duties, preached before the University of Dublin; being the Donnellan Lectures for 1860. 8vo. 6s.

Barrow's (Dr. Isaac) Works; compared with the Original MSS. and enlarged with Materials hitherto unpublished. A New Edition, by A. Napier, M.A., of Trinity College, Vicar of Holkham, Norfolk. 9 vols. 8vo. 4l. 14s. 6d.

Battle (The) Won. An Epic Poem. By a Carthusian. 8vo. 10s. 6d.

Bean's (Rev. James) Family Worship; a Course of Morning and Evening Prayers for every Day in the Month. Twentieth Edition. Small 8vo. 4s. 6d.

Beaven's (Rev. Dr.) Help to Catechising; for the use of Clergymen, Schools, and Private Families. New Edition. 18mo. 2s.

Berens's (Archdeacon) Thirty-three Village Sermons, on the chief Articles of Faith, and the Means of Grace, on certain Parts of the Christian Character, and on some of the Relative Duties. New Edition. 12mo. 4s. 6d.

―――――――――――― Selection from the Papers of Addison in the Spectator and Guardian; for the Use of Young Persons. New Edition. 12mo. 4s. 6d.

―――――――――――― Christmas Stories. Contents:―Good Nature― The Smuggler ― Village Politics ― and Robin Goodfellow. Seventh Edition. Small 8vo. 3s.

Bethell's (late Bp. of Bangor) General View of the Doctrine of Regeneration in Baptism. Fifth Edition. 8vo. 9s.

Bickersteth's (Archdeacon) Questions illustrating the Thirty-nine Articles of the Church of England: with Proofs from Scripture and the Primitive Church. Fourth Edition. 12mo. 3s. 6d.

―――――――――――― Catechetical Exercises on the Apostles' Creed; chiefly drawn from the Exposition of Bishop Pearson. New Edition. 18mo. 2s.

Boyle's (W. R. A.) Inspiration of the Book of Daniel, and other portions of Sacred Scripture. With a correction of Profane, and an adjustment of Sacred Chronology. 8vo. 14s.

Bray's (Rev. E. A.) Sermons, General and Occasional. 2 vols. small 8vo. 14s.

Brown's (Rev. G. J.) Lectures on the Gospel according to St. John, in the form of a Continuous Commentary. 2 vols. 8vo. 24s.

Brown (Rev. Stafford), Memoir of, with Extracts from his Diary and Sermons. By his Widow. Crown 8vo. 3s. 6d.

Browne's (Sir Thomas) Christian Morals. With a Life of the Author by Samuel Johnson. In small 8vo. with Portrait of Author, price 6s. handsomely printed on toned paper from antique type.

Burke.—A Complete Edition of the Works and Correspondence of the Right Hon. Edmund Burke. In 8 vols. 8vo. *With Portrait.* 4l. 4s.

Contents:—1. Mr. Burke's Correspondence between the year 1744 and his Decease in 1797, first published from the original MSS. in 1844, edited by Earl Fitzwilliam and Sir Richard Bourke. The most interesting portion of the Letters of Mr. Burke to Dr. French Laurence is also included in it.

2. The Works of Mr. Burke, as edited by his Literary Executors, and completed by the publication of the 15th and 16th Volumes, in 1826, under the Superintendence of the late Bishop of Rochester, Dr. Walker King.

Burke's (Edmund) Reflections on the Revolution in France, in 1790. New Edition, with a short Biographical Notice. 8vo. 4s. 6d.

Byng's (Rev. F. E. C.) Sermons for Households. Crown 8vo. 3s. 6d.

Caswall's (Rev. Dr.) Martyr of the Pongas. A Memoir of the Rev. Hamble James Leacock, first West-Indian Missionary to Western Africa. Small 8vo. With Portrait. 5s. 6d.

Chevallier's (Rev. Professor) Translation of the Epistles of Clemens Romanus, Ignatius, and Polycarp, and of the Apologies of Justin Martyr and Tertullian. With Notes, and an Account of the Present State of the Question respecting the Epistles of Ignatius. Second Edition. 8vo. 12s.

Christian's (The) Duty, from the Sacred Scriptures. In Two Parts. Part I. Exhortation to Repentance and a Holy Life. Part II. Devotions for the Closet, in Three Offices, for every Day in the Week. [*London: sold by C. Rivington, in St. Paul's Churchyard.* 1730.] New Edition. Edited by the Rev. Thomas Dale, M.A. Small 8vo. (1852.) 5s.

Clabon's (John M.) Praise, Precept, and Prayer; a Complete Manual of Family Worship. Part I. From the Old Testament, for Morning use. Part II. From the Old and New Testaments, and from the best Commentators, for Evening use. Part III. From "The Imitation of Christ." Part IV. Prayers for Six Weeks. 8vo. 16s.

Clergy Charities.—List of Charities, General and Diocesan, for the Relief of the Clergy, their Widows and Families. Fifth Edition. Small 8vo. 3s.

Clissold's (Rev. H.) Lamps of the Church; or, Rays of Faith, Hope, and Charity, from the Lives and Deaths of some Eminent Christians of the Nineteenth Century. Crown 8vo., *with five Portraits on Steel*, 9s. 6d. *In morocco*, 15s.

Cottager's Monthly Visitor.—Thirty-six Volumes of this Work have been published, forming a Repository of Religious Instruction and Domestic Economy, suited to Family Reading, the Parochial Library, and the Servants' Hall. Its contents include Spiritual Exposition, Instructive Tales, Hints on Gardening and Agriculture, and short Extracts from the best Authors. All the volumes are sold separately, 4s. *each*.

Cotterill's Selection of Psalms and Hymns for Public Worship. New and cheaper Editions. 32mo., 1s.; in 18mo. (large print), 1s. 6d. Also an Edition on fine paper, 2s. 6d.

*** A large allowance to Clergymen and Churchwardens.

Crosthwaite's (Rev. J. C.) Historical Passages and Characters in the Book of Daniel; Eight Lectures, delivered in 1852, at the Lecture founded by the late Bernard Hyde, Esq. To which are added, Four Discourses on Mutual Recognition in a Future State. 12mo. 7s. 6d.

Davys's (Bp. of Peterborough) Plain and Short History of England for Children: in Letters from a Father to his Son. With Questions. Thirteenth Edition. 18mo. 2s. 6d.

——————————— **Volume for a Lending Library**; chiefly selected from the *Cottager's Monthly Visitor*. Small 8vo. 4s. 6d.

Early Influences. By the Author of "Truth without Prejudice." Third Edition. Small 8vo. 3s. 6d.

Ellison's (Rev. H. J.) Way of Holiness in Married Life; a Course of Sermons preached in Lent. Second Edition. Small 8vo. 2s. 6d. *In white cloth, antique style*, 3s. 6d.

Evans's (Archdeacon) Scripture Biography. In 3 vols. small 8vo. 18s.

——————————— **Biography of the Early Church.** Second Edition. 2 vols. small 8vo. 12s.

——————————— **Bishopric of Souls.** Fourth Edition. Small 8vo. 5s.

Evans's (Archdeacon) Ministry of the Body. Second Edition. Small 8vo. 6s. 6d.

Exton's (Rev. R. B.) Speculum Gregis ; or, the Parochial Minister's Assistant in the Oversight of his Flock. With blank forms to be filled up at discretion. Seventh Edition. In pocket size. 4s. 6d. bound with clasp.

Fearon's (Rev. H.) Sermons on Public Subjects. Small 8vo. 3s. 6d.

Galloway's (Rev. W. B.) Clergyman's Holidays: or, Friendly Discussions, Historical, Scriptural, and Philosophical. Small 8vo. 5s.

———————————— **Ezekiel's Sign, Metrically Para-**phrased and Interpreted, from his Fourth and Fifth Chapters; with Notes and Elucidations. Small 8vo. 2s. 6d.

Giles's (Rev. J. D.) Village Sermons preached at some of the chief Christian Seasons, in the Parish Church of Belleau with Aby. Small 8vo. 5s.

Gilly's (late Canon) Memoir of Felix Neff, Pastor of the High Alps; and of his Labours among the French Protestants of Dauphiné, a Remnant of the Primitive Christians of Gaul. Sixth Edition. Fcap. 5s. 6d.

Girdlestone's (Rev. Charles) Holy Bible, containing the Old and New Testaments; with a Commentary arranged in Short Lectures for the Daily Use of Families. New Edition, in 6 vols. 8vo. 3l. 3s.

    The Old Testament separately. 4 vols. 8vo. 42s.
    The New Testament. 2 vols. 8vo. 21s.

Goulburn's (Rev. Dr.) Thoughts on Personal Religion. Fourth Edition, enlarged. Small 8vo. 6s. 6d.

*** The two additional Chapters have been printed separately, price 6d.

——————————— **Office of the Holy Communion in** the Book of Common Prayer; a Series of Lectures delivered in the Church of St. John the Evangelist, Paddington. 2 vols. small 8vo. 10s. 6d.

——————————— **Sermons preached on Various Occa-**sions during the last Twenty Years. Second Edition. 2 vols. small 8vo. 10s. 6d.

——————————— **Manual of Confirmation ;** comprising a General Account of the Ordinance, the English Order of Confirmation with Notes, and Meditations and Prayers: with a Pastoral Letter on First Communion. Fourth Edition. 1s. 6d.

——————————— **Introduction to the Devotional** Study of the Holy Scriptures. Fifth Edition. Small 8vo. 4s. 6d.

——————————— **Family Prayers, arranged on the** Liturgical Principle. Small 8vo. 3s.

Green.—Brief Memorials of the late Rev. Charles Green, M.A., of Worcester College, Oxford; Missionary and Secretary of the Society for the Propagation of the Gospel. Small 8vo. 2s. 6d.

Greswell's (Rev. Edward) The Three Witnesses and the Threefold Cord; being the Testimony of the Natural Measures of Time, of the Primitive Civil Calendar, and of Antediluvian and Postdiluvian Tradition, on the Principal Questions of Fact in Sacred or Profane Antiquity. 8vo. 7s. 6d.

——————————— Objections to the Historical Character of the Pentateuch, in Part I. of Dr. Colenso's "Pentateuch and Book of Joshua," considered, and shown to be unfounded. 8vo. 5s.

——————————— Exposition of the Parables and of other Parts of the Gospels. 5 vols. (in 6 parts), 8vo. 3l. 12s.

Grotius de Veritate Religionis Christianæ. With English Notes and Illustrations, for the use of Students. By the Rev. J. E. Middleton, M.A., of Trinity College, Cambridge; Lecturer on Theology at St. Bees' College. Second Edition. 12mo. 6s.

Gurney's (Rev. J. H.) Sermons on the Acts of the Apostles. With a Preface by the Dean of Canterbury. Small 8vo. 7s.

——————————— Sermons chiefly on Old Testament Histories, from Texts in the Sunday Lessons. Second Edition. 6s.

——————————— Sermons on Texts from the Epistles and Gospels for Twenty Sundays. Second Edition. 6s.

——————————— Miscellaneous Sermons. 6s.

Hale's (Archdeacon) Sick Man's Guide to Acts of Faith, Patience, Charity, and Repentance. Extracted from Bishop Taylor's Holy Dying. In large print. Second Edition. 8vo. 3s.

Hall's (Rev. W. J.) Psalms and Hymns adapted to the Services of the Church of England; with a Supplement of additional Hymns and Indices. In 8vo., 8s.—18mo., 3s.—24mo., 1s. 6d.—24mo., limp cloth, 1s. 3d.—24mo., fine paper, 2s.—32mo., 1s.—32mo., limp, 8d.—32mo., fine paper, 2s. (The Supplement may be had separately.)

——————————— Selection of Tunes. Royal 8vo., 12s. Oblong 12mo., 3s. 6d.

*** A Prospectus of the above, with Specimens of Type, and farther particulars, may be had of the Publishers.

Hawkins's (Rev. W. B.) Limits of Religious Belief: Suggestions addressed to the Student in Divine Things. Small 8vo. 2s. 6d.

Help and Comfort for the Sick Poor. By the Author of "Sickness: its Trials and Blessings." Fourth Edition, *in large print*. 1s., or 1s. 6d. *in cloth*.

Henley's (Hon. and Rev. R.) The Prayer of Prayers. Small 8vo. 4s. 6d.

Hey's (John) Lectures on Divinity, delivered in the University of Cambridge. Third Edition, by T. Turton, D.D., Lord Bishop of Ely. 2 vols. 8vo. 30s.

Heygate's (Rev. W. E.) Care of the Soul; or, Sermons on Points of Christian Prudence. 12mo. 5s. 6d.

——————————— **The Good Shepherd;** or, Christ the Pattern, Priest, and Pastor. 18mo. 3s. 6d.

Hodgson's (Chr.) Instructions for the Use of Candidates for Holy Orders, and of the Parochial Clergy, as to Ordination, Licences, Induction, Pluralities, Residence, &c. &c.; with Acts of Parliament relating to the above, and Forms to be used. Eighth Edition, revised and corrected. 8vo. 12s.

Holden's (Rev. Geo.) Ordinance of Preaching investigated. Small 8vo. 3s. 6d.

——————————— **Christian Expositor;** or, Practical Guide to the Study of the New Testament. Intended for the use of General Readers. Second Edition. 12mo. 12s.

Holy Thoughts; or, A Treasury of True Riches. Collected chiefly from our Old Writers. Eighth Edition. 1s. 6d.

Homilies (The) with Various Readings, and the Quotations from the Fathers given at length in the Original Languages. Edited by G. E. Corrie, D.D. 8vo. 10s. 6d.

Hook's (Dean) Book of Family Prayer. Sixth Edition. 18mo. 2s.

——————————— **Private Prayers.** Fifth Edition. 18mo. 2s.

——————————— **Dictionary of Ecclesiastical Biography.** 8 vols. 12mo. 2l. 11s.

Hooper's (Rev. F. B.) Exposition of the Revelations. 2 vols. 8vo. 28s.

Hulton's (Rev. C. G.) Catechetical Help to Bishop Butler's Analogy. Third Edition. Post 8vo. 4s. 6d.

Hymns and Poems for the Sick and Suffering; in connexion with the Service for the Visitation of the Sick. Selected from various Authors. Edited by the Rev. T. V. Fosbery, M.A., Vicar of St. Giles's, Reading. Fifth Edition. 5s. 6d. in cloth, or 9s. 6d. in morocco.

> This Volume contains 233 separate pieces; of which about 90 are by writers who lived prior to the 18th Century; the rest are modern, and some of these original. Amongst the names of the writers (between 70 and 80 in number) occur those of Sir J. Beaumont—Sir T. Browne—Elizabeth of Bohemia—Phineas Fletcher—George Herbert—Dean Hickes—Bp. Ken—Quarles—Sandys—Jeremy Taylor—Henry Vaughan—and Sir H. Wotton. And of modern writers—Mrs. Barrett Browning—Bishop Wilberforce—S. T. Coleridge—W. Wordsworth—Dean Trench—Rev. Messrs. Chandler—Keble—Lyte—Monsell—and Moultrie.

Jackson's (Bp. of Lincoln) Six Sermons on the Christian Character; preached in Lent. Seventh Edition. Small 8vo. 3s. 6d.

James's (Rev. Dr.) Comment upon the Collects appointed to be used in the Church of England on Sundays and Holydays throughout the Year. Fifteenth Edition. 12mo. 5s.

——————— **Christian Watchfulness in the Prospect** of Sickness, Mourning, and Death. Eighth Edition. 12mo. 6s.

Cheap Editions of these two works may be had, price 3s. each.

——————— **Evangelical Life, as seen in the Ex-** ample of our Lord Jesus Christ. Second Edition. 12mo. 7s. 6d.

——————— **Devotional Comment on the Morn-** ing and Evening Services in the Book of Common Prayer, in a Series of Plain Lectures. Second Edition. In 2 vols. 12mo. 10s. 6d.

Inman's (Rev. Professor) Treatise on Navigation and Nautical Astronomy, for the Use of British Seamen. Thirteenth Edition, edited by the Rev. J. W. Inman. Royal 8vo. 7s.

——————— **Nautical Tables for the Use** of British Seamen. New Edition, edited by the Rev. J. W. Inman. Royal 8vo. 14s.

Kaye's (late Bp. of Lincoln) Account of the Writings and Opinions of Justin Martyr. Third Edition. 8vo. 7s. 6d.

——————— **Ecclesiastical History of the** Second and Third Centuries, Illustrated from the Writings of Tertullian. Third Edition. 8vo. 13s.

——————— **Account of the Writings and** Opinions of Clement of Alexandria. 8vo. 12s.

——————— **Account of the Council of** Nicæa, in connexion with the Life of Athanasius. 8vo. 8s.

Kennaway's (Rev. C. E.) Consolatio; or, Comfort for the Afflicted. Selected from various Authors. With a Preface by the Bishop of Oxford. Tenth Edition. Small 8vo. 4s. 6d.

Knowles's (Rev. E. H.) Notes on the Epistle to the He- brews, with Analysis and Brief Paraphrase; for Theological Students. Crown 8vo. 6s. 6d.

Landon's (Rev. E. H.) Manual of Councils of the Holy Catholic Church, comprising the Substance of the most Remarkable and Important Canons. Alphabetically arranged. 12mo. 12s.

Latin Reader.—De Viris Illustribus Urbis Romæ, a Romulo ad Augustum. An Elementary Latin Reading Book, being a Series of Biographical Chapters on Roman History, chronologically arranged. By the Editor of the " Graduated Series of English Reading Books." Small 8vo. 3s.

Lee's (Rev. Professor) Inspiration of Holy Scripture, its
Nature and Proof: Eight Discourses preached before the University of
Dublin. Second Edition, revised, with Index. 8vo. 14s.

McCaul's (Rev. Dr.) Testimonies to the Divine Authority
and Inspiration of Holy Scripture, as taught by the Church of England.
Crown 8vo. 4s. 6d.

────────── **Examination of Bp. Colenso's Diffi-**
culties with regard to the Pentateuch; and some Reasons for believing in
its Authenticity and Divine Origin. Third Library Edition. Crown
8vo. 5s.   Also, the PEOPLE'S EDITION, *ninth thousand*, price 1s.

Macdonnell's (Dean of Cashel) Donnellan Lectures on the
Doctrine of the Atonement. 8vo. 7s.

Mackenzie's (Rev. H.) Ordination Lectures, delivered in
Riseholme Palace Chapel, during Ember Weeks. Small 8vo. 3s.
   Contents:—Pastoral Government—Educational Work—Self-govern-
ment in the Pastor—Missions and their Reflex Results—Dissent—Public
Teaching—Sunday Schools—Doctrinal Controversy—Secular Aids.

Maitland's (Rev. Dr.) Voluntary System; in a Series of
Letters. 12mo. 6s. 6d.

────────── **Dark Ages: a Series of Essays in**
illustration of the Religion and Literature of the Ninth, Tenth, Eleventh,
and Twelfth Centuries. Third Edition. 8vo. 12s.

────────── **Essays on Subjects connected with**
the Reformation in England. 8vo. 15s.

Mant's (late Bishop) Book of Common Prayer and Adminis-
tration of the Sacraments, with copious Notes, Practical and Historical,
from approved Writers of the Church of England; including the Canons
and Constitutions of the Church. New Edition. In one volume, super-
royal 8vo. 24s.

────────── **Happiness of the Blessed considered as to**
the Particulars of their State; their Recognition of each other in that
State; and its Difference of Degrees. Seventh Edition. 12mo. 4s.

Margaret Stourton; or, a Year of Governess Life. Ele-
gantly printed in small 8vo. Price 5s.

Markby's (Rev. Thomas) The Man Christ Jesus; or, the
Daily Life, and Teaching of our Lord, in Childhood and Manhood, on
Earth. Crown 8vo. 9s. 6d.

Marsh's (late Bp. of Peterborough) Comparative View of the
Churches of England and Rome: with an Appendix on Church Authority,
the Character of Schism, and the Rock on which our Saviour declared
that He would build His Church. Third Edition. Small 8vo. 6s.

Melvill's (Rev. H.) Sermons. Vol. I., Sixth Edition. Vol.
II., Fourth Edition. 10s. 6d. *each*.

────────── **Sermons on some of the less prominent**
Facts and References in Sacred Story. Second Edition. 2 vols. 8vo.
10s. 6d. *each*.

MESSRS. RIVINGTON'S CATALOGUE. 11

Melvill's (Rev. H.) Selection from the Lectures delivered
at St. Margaret's, Lothbury, on the Tuesday Mornings in the Years 1850,
1851, 1852. Small 8vo. 6s.

Middleton's (Bp.) Doctrine of the Greek Article applied
to the Criticism and Illustration of the New Testament. By the late
Bishop Middleton. With Prefatory Observations and Notes, by Hugh
James Rose, B.D., late Principal of King's College, London. New
Edition. In 8vo. 12s.

Mill's (Rev. Dr.) Analysis of Bishop Pearson on the Creed.
Third Edition. 8vo. 5s.

Miller's (Rev. J. K.) Parochial Sermons. Small 8vo. 4s. 6d.

Monsell's (Rev. Dr.) Parish Musings; or, Devotional Poems.
Sixth Edition, elegantly printed on toned paper. Small 8vo. 2s. 6d.
Also, a CHEAP EDITION, price 1s. sewed, or 1s. 6d. in limp cloth.

Moon's (R.) Pentateuch and the Book of Joshua considered
with Reference to the Objections of the Bishop of Natal. 8vo. 6s.

Moreton's (Rev. Julian) Life and Work in Newfoundland:
Reminiscences of Thirteen Years spent there. Crown 8vo., *with a Map
and four Illustrations.* 5s. 6d.

Mozley's (Rev. J. B.) Review of the Baptismal Controversy.
8vo. 9s. 6d.

Nixon's (Bishop) Lectures, Historical, Doctrinal, and Practical, on the Catechism of the Church of England. Sixth Edition.
8vo. 18s.

O'Keeffe's (Miss) Patriarchal Times; or, The Land of
Canaan: in Seven Books. Comprising interesting Events, Incidents, and
Characters, founded on the Holy Scriptures. Seventh Edition. Small
8vo. 6s. 6d.

Old Man's (The) Rambles. Sixth and cheaper Edition.
18mo. 3s. 6d.

Page's (Rev. J. R.) Pretensions of Bishop Colenso to impeach
the Wisdom and Veracity of the Compilers of the Holy Scriptures considered. 8vo. 5s.

Palmer's (Rev. W.) Origines Liturgicæ; or, the Antiquities
of the English Ritual: with a Dissertation on Primitive Liturgies.
Fourth Edition, enlarged. 2 vols. 8vo. 18s.

Parkinson's (Canon) Old Church Clock. Fourth Edition.
Small 8vo. 4s. 6d.

Parry's (Mrs.) Young Christian's Sunday Evening; or,
Conversations on Scripture History. In 3 vols. small 8vo. Sold
separately:
First Series: on the Old Testament. Fourth Edition. 6s. 6d.
Second Series: on the Gospels. Third Edition. 7s.
Third Series: on the Acts. Second Edition. 4s. 6d.

Pearson's Exposition of the Creed; edited by Temple Chevallier, B.D., Professor of Mathematics in the University of Durham, and late Fellow and Tutor of St. Catharine's College, Cambridge. Second Edition. 8vo. 10s. 6d.

Peile's (Rev. Dr.) Annotations on the Apostolical Epistles. New Edition. 4 vols. 8vo. 42s.

Penny Sunday Reader.—This Work, first published in Numbers, consists of 14 volumes (sold separately, price 2s. 9d. each), and contains a plain, popular, and copious Commentary on the Book of Common Prayer; besides numerous Devotional Essays, Sacred Poetry, and Extracts from Eminent Divines. The earlier volumes were edited by the Rev. Dr. Molesworth, Vicar of Rochdale, and the whole Series is included in the List of Books recommended by the Society for Promoting Christian Knowledge.

Pepys's (Lady C.) Quiet Moments: a Four Weeks' Course of Thoughts and Meditations before Evening Prayer and at Sunset. Fourth Edition. Small 8vo. 3s. 6d.

——————————— **Morning Notes of Praise:** a Companion Volume. Second Edition. 3s. 6d.

——————————— **Thoughts for the Hurried and Hardworking.** Second Edition, in large print, price 1s. sewed, or 1s. 6d. in limp cloth.

Pinder's (Rev. J. H.) Sermons on the Book of Common Prayer and Administration of the Sacraments. To which are now added, Several Sermons on the Feasts and Fasts of the Church, preached in the Cathedral Church of Wells. Third Edition. 12mo. 7s.

——————————— **Sermons on the Holy Days observed in the Church of England throughout the Year.** Second Edition. 12mo. 6s. 6d.

——————————— **Meditations and Prayers on the Ordination Service for Deacons.** Small 8vo. 3s. 6d.

——————————— **Meditations and Prayers on the Ordination Service for Priests.** Small 8vo. 3s. 6d.

Plain Sermons. By Contributors to the "Tracts for the Times." In 10 vols. 8vo., 6s. 6d. each. (Sold separately.)

This Series contains 347 original Sermons of moderate length, written in simple language, and in an earnest and impressive style, forming a copious body of practical Theology, in accordance with the Doctrines of the Church of England. They are particularly suited for family reading. The last Volume contains a general Index of Subjects, and a Table of the Sermons adapted to the various Seasons of the Christian Year.

Prayers for the Sick and Dying. By the Author of "Sickness, its Trials and Blessings." Third Edition. Small 8vo. 2s. 6d.

Reminiscences by a Clergyman's Wife. Edited by the Dean of Canterbury. Second Edition. Crown 8vo. 3s. 6d.

Schmitz's (Dr. L.) Manual of Ancient History, from the
Remotest Times to the Overthrow of the Western Empire, A.D. 476.
Third Edition. Crown 8vo. 7s. 6d.
This Work, for the convenience of Schools, may be had in Two Parts,
sold separately, viz.—
Vol. I., containing, besides the History of India and the other Asiatic
Nations, a complete History of Greece. 4s.
Vol. II., containing a complete History of Rome. 4s.

——————————— Manual of Ancient Geography. Crown
8vo. 6s.

——————————— History of the Middle Ages. In 2
vols. Vol. I. (from the Downfall of the Western Empire, A.D. 476, to
the Crusades, A.D. 1096.) Crown 8vo. 7s. 6d.

Seymour's (Rev. R.) and Mackarness's (Rev. J. F.) Eighteen
Years of a Clerical Meeting: being the Minutes of the Alcester Clerical
Association, from 1842 to 1860; with a Preface on the Revival of Ruri-
decanal Chapters. Crown 8vo. 6s. 6d.

Shuttleworth's (late Bp. of Chichester) Paraphrastic Translation of the Apostolical Epistles, with Notes. Fifth Edition. 8vo. 9s.

Sickness, its Trials and Blessings. Seventh Edition. Small
8vo. 5s. Also, a cheaper Edition, for distribution, 2s. 6d.

Slade's (late Canon) Annotations on the Epistles; being a
Continuation of Mr. Elsley's "Annotations on the Four Gospels and Acts
of the Apostles." Fifth Edition. 2 vols. 8vo. 18s.

——————————— Twenty-one Prayers composed from
the Psalms for the Sick and Afflicted: with other Forms of Prayer, and
Hints and Directions for the Visitation of the Sick. Seventh Edition.
12mo. 3s. 6d.

——————————— Plain Parochial Sermons. 7 vols. 12mo.
6s. each. (Sold separately.)

Smith's (John) Select Discourses. Edited by H. G. Williams, B.D., Professor of Arabic in the University of Cambridge.
Royal 8vo. 10s. 6d.

Smith's (Rev. Dr. J. B.) Manual of the Rudiments of
Theology: containing an Abridgment of Tomline's Elements; an Analysis
of Paley's Evidences; a Summary of Pearson on the Creed; and a brief
Exposition of the Thirty-nine Articles, chiefly from Burnet; Explanation
of Jewish Rites and Ceremonies, &c. &c. Fifth Edition. 12mo. 8s. 6d.

——————————— Compendium of Rudiments in
Theology: containing a Digest of Bishop Butler's Analogy; an Epitome
of Dean Graves on the Pentateuch; and an Analysis of Bishop Newton
on the Prophecies. Second Edition. 12mo. 9s.

Sneyd's (Miss C. A.) Meditations for a Month, on Select
Passages of Scripture. Small 8vo. 3s. 6d.

Tait's (Rev. W.) Seeds of Thought. Crown 8vo. 4s. 6d.

Talbot's (Hon. Mrs. J. C.) Parochial Mission-Women; their Work and its Fruits. Second Edition. Small 8vo. *In limp cloth*, 2s.

Thornton's (Rev. T.) Life of Moses, in a Course of Village
Lectures; with a Preface Critical of Bishop Colenso's Work on the Pentateuch. Small 8vo. 3s. 6d.

Threshold (The) of Private Devotion. 18mo. 2s.

Townsend's (Canon) Holy Bible, containing the Old and
New Testaments, arranged in Historical and Chronological Order, so that the whole may be read as one connected History, in the words of the Authorized Translation. With copious Notes and Indexes. Fifth Edition. In 2 vols., imperial 8vo., 21s. *each* (sold separately).

Also, an Edition of this Arrangement of the Bible without the Notes, in One Volume, 14s.

——————————— **Scriptural Communion with God;**
or, the Pentateuch and the Book of Job, arranged in Historical and Chronological Order, and newly divided into sections for daily reading; with Introductions and Prayers, and Notes for the Student and Inquirer. In 2 large vols. 8vo. 45s.

Trimmer's (the late Mrs.) Abridgment of Scripture History; consisting of Lessons from the Old Testament. New Edition. 12mo. 1s. 6d.

——————————— **Abridgment of the New Testament;** consisting of Lessons from the Writings of the Four Evangelists. New Edition. 12mo. 1s. 4d.

Trollope's (Rev. W.) Iliad of Homer from a carefully corrected Text; with copious English Notes, illustrating the Grammatical Construction, the Manners and Customs, the Mythology and Antiquities of the Heroic Ages; and Preliminary Observations on points of Classical interest. Fifth Edition. 8vo. 15s.

——————————— **Excerpta ex Ovidii Metam. et Epistolæ.**
With English Notes, and an Introduction, containing Rules for Construing, a Parsing Praxis, &c. Third Edition. 12mo. 3s. 6d.

——————————— **Bellum Catilinarium of Sallust, and**
Cicero's Four Orations against Catiline; with English Notes and Introduction. Together with the Bellum Jugurthinum of Sallust. Third Edition. 12mo. 3s. 6d.

Truth without Prejudice. Fourth Edition. Small 8vo. 3s. 6d.

Twelve (The) Churches; or, Tracings along the Watling
Street. By the Author of "The Red Rose." With Eight Lithographic Plates. Royal 8vo. 3s. 6d.

Vidal's (Mrs.) Tales for the Bush. Originally published in Australia. Fourth Edition. Small 8vo. 5s.

Warter's (Rev. J. W.) The Sea-board and the Down; or, My Parish in the South. In 2 vols. small 4to. Elegantly printed in Antique type, with Illustrations. 28s.

—————————— Plain Practical Sermons. 2 vols. 8vo. 26s.

—————————— Teaching of the Prayer-book. 8vo. 7s. 6d.

Welchman's Thirty-nine Articles of the Church of England, illustrated with Notes, and confirmed by Texts of Holy Scripture, and Testimonies of the Primitive Fathers; with references to passages in the writings of various Divines. Fifteenth Edition. 8vo. 2s. Or, interleaved with blank paper, 3s.

Wheatly on the Common Prayer; edited by G. E. Corrie, D.D., Master of Jesus College, Examining Chaplain to the Lord Bishop of Ely. 8vo. 10s. 6d.

Wilberforce's (Bp. of Oxford) History of the Protestant Episcopal Church in America. Third Edition. Small 8vo. 5s.

—————————— Rocky Island, and other Similitudes. Twelfth Edition, with Cuts. 18mo. 2s. 6d.

—————————— Sermons preached before the Queen. Sixth Edition. 12mo. 6s.

—————————— Selection of Psalms and Hymns for Public Worship. New Edition. 32mo. 1s. each, or 3l. 10s. per hundred.

Williams's (Rev. Isaac) Devotional Commentary on the Gospel Narrative. 8 vols. small 8vo. 3l. 6s.

Sold separately as follows :—

Thoughts on the Study of the Gospels. 8s.
Harmony of the Evangelists. 8s. 6d.
The Nativity (extending to the Calling of St. Matthew). 8s. 6d.
Second Year of the Ministry. 8s.
Third Year of the Ministry. 8s. 6d.
The Holy Week. 8s. 6d.   The Passion. 8s.
The Resurrection. 8s.

—————————— Apocalypse, with Notes and Reflections. Small 8vo. 8s. 6d.

—————————— Beginning of the Book of Genesis, with Notes and Reflections. Small 8vo. 7s. 6d.

—————————— Sermons on the Characters of the Old Testament. Second Edition. 5s. 6d.

Williams's (Rev. Isaac) Female Characters of Holy Scripture; in a Series of Sermons. Second Edition. Small 8vo. 5s. 6d.

—————————————— Plain Sermons on the Latter Part of the Catechism; being the Conclusion of the Series contained in the Ninth Volume of "Plain Sermons." 8vo. 6s. 6d.

—————————————— Complete Series of Sermons on the Catechism. In one Volume. 13s.

—————————————— Sermons on the Epistle and Gospel for the Sundays and Holy Days throughout the Year. Second Edition. In 3 vols. small 8vo. 16s. 6d.

*** The Third Volume, on the Saints' Days and other Holy Days of the Church, may be had separately, price 5s. 6d.

—————————————— Christian Seasons; a Series of Poems. Small 8vo. 3s. 6d.

Wilson's (late Bp. of Sodor and Man) Short and Plain Instruction for the Better Understanding of the Lord's Supper. To which is annexed, The Office of the Holy Communion, with Proper Helps and Directions. Pocket size, 1s. Also, a larger Edition, 2s.

—————————————— Sacra Privata; Private Meditations and Prayers. Pocket size, 1s. Also, a larger Edition, 2s.

These two Works may be had in various bindings.

Wordsworth's (late Rev. Dr.) Ecclesiastical Biography; or, Lives of Eminent Men connected with the History of Religion in England, from the Commencement of the Reformation to the Revolution. Selected, and Illustrated with Notes. Fourth Edition. In 4 vols. 8vo. With 5 Portraits. 2l. 14s.

Wordsworth's (Bp. of St. Andrew's) Christian Boyhood at a Public School: a Collection of Sermons and Lectures delivered at Winchester College from 1836 to 1846. In 2 vols. 8vo. 1l. 4s.

—————————————— Catechesis; or, Christian Instruction preparatory to Confirmation and First Communion. Third Edition. Crown 8vo. 3s. 6d.

Wordsworth's (Canon) New Testament of our Lord and Saviour Jesus Christ, in the original Greek. With Notes, Introductions, and Indexes. New Edition. In Two Vols., imperial 8vo. 4l.

Separately,

Part I.: The Four Gospels. 1l. 1s.
Part II.: The Acts of the Apostles. 10s. 6d.
Part III.: The Epistles of St. Paul. 1l. 11s. 6d.
Part IV.: The General Epistles and Book of Revelation; with Indexes, 1l. 1s.

Wordsworth's (Canon) Occasional Sermons preached in Westminster Abbey. In 7 vols. 8vo. Vols. I., II., and III., 7s. each—Vols. IV. and V., 8s. each—Vol. VI., 7s.—Vol. VII., 6s.

—————— **Theophilus Anglicanus;** or, Instruction concerning the Principles of the Church Universal and the Church of England. New Edition. 5s.

—————— **Elements of Instruction on the Church**; being an Abridgment of the above. Second Edition. 2s.

—————— **Journal of a Tour in Italy;** with Reflections on the Present Condition and Prospects of Religion in that Country. Second Edition. 2 vols. post 8vo. 15s.

—————— **On the Inspiration of the Bible.** Five Lectures delivered at Westminster Abbey. New and cheaper Edition. 1s.

—————— **On the Interpretation of the Bible.** Five Lectures delivered at Westminster Abbey. 3s. 6d.

—————— **S. Hippolytus and the Church of Rome** in the beginning of the Third Century, from the newly-discovered "Philosophumena." 8s. 6d.

—————— **Letters to M. Gondon,** Author of "Mouvement Religieux en Angleterre," on the Destructive Character of the Church of Rome, in Religion and Polity. Third Edition. 7s. 6d.

—————— **Sequel to the Above.** Second Edition. 6s. 6d.

—————— **On the Canon of Holy Scripture** and on the Apocrypha. Twelve Discourses, preached before the University of Cambridge. With a copious Appendix of Ancient Authorities. Second Edition. 9s.

—————— **Lectures on the Apocalypse;** preached before the University of Cambridge. Third Edition. 10s. 6d.

—————— **Holy Year:** Hymns for Sundays and Holydays, and for other Occasions; with a preface on Hymnology. Third Edition, in larger type, square 16mo., cloth extra, 4s. 6d. Also a cheaper Edition, 2s. 6d.

Yonge's (C. D.) History of England from the Earliest Times to the Peace of Paris, 1856. With a Chronological Table of Contents. In one thick volume, crown 8vo. 12s.

> Though available as a School-book, this volume contains as much as three ordinary octavos. It is written on a carefully digested plan, ample space being given to the last three centuries. All the best authorities have been consulted.

Arnold's Practical Introductions to Greek, Latin, &c.

Henry's First Latin Book. Seventeenth Edition, carefully revised. 12mo. 3s.

The object of this work is to enable the youngest boys to master the principal difficulties of the Latin language by easy steps, and to furnish older students with a Manual for Self-Tuition.

In the present Edition great attention has been given to the improvement of what may be called its mechanical parts. The Vocabularies have been much extended, and greater uniformity of reference has been secured. A few rules have been omitted or simplified. Every thing has been done which the long experience of the Editor, or the practice of his friends in their own schools has shown to be desirable.

At the same time, no pains have been spared to do this without altering in any way the character of the work, or making it inconvenient to use it side by side with copies of the last edition.

A Second Latin Book, and Practical Grammar. Intended as a Sequel to Henry's First Latin Book. Seventh Edition. 12mo. 4s.

A First Verse Book, Part I.; intended as an easy Introduction to the Latin Hexameter and Pentameter. Seventh Edition. 12mo. 2s.

A First Verse Book, Part II.; containing additional Exercises. Second Edition. 1s.

Historiæ Antiquæ Epitome, from *Cornelius Nepos, Justin*, &c. With English Notes, Rules for Construing, Questions, Geographical Lists, &c. Seventh Edition. 4s.

A First Classical Atlas, containing fifteen Maps, coloured in outline; intended as a Companion to the *Historiæ Antiquæ Epitome*. 8vo. 7s. 6d.

A Practical Introduction to Latin Prose Composition. Part I. Eleventh Edition. 8vo. 6s. 6d.

This Work is founded on the principles of imitation and frequent repetition. It is at once a Syntax, a Vocabulary, and an Exercise Book; and considerable attention has been paid to the subject of Synonymes. It is now used at all, or nearly all, the public schools.

MESSRS. RIVINGTON'S CATALOGUE. 19

A Practical Introduction to Latin Prose Composition, Part II.; containing the Doctrine of Latin Particles, with Vocabulary, an Antibarbarus, &c. Fourth Edition. 8vo. 8s.

A Practical Introduction to Latin Verse Composition. 8vo. Third Edition. 5s. 6d.

Contents:—1. "Ideas" for Hexameter and Elegiac Verses. 2. Alcaics. 3. Sapphics. 4. The other Horatian Metres. 5. Appendix of Poetical Phraseology, and Hints on Versification.

Gradus ad Parnassum Novus Anticlepticus; founded on Quicherat's *Thesaurus Poeticus Linguæ Latinæ*. 8vo. *half-bound*. 10s. 6d.

⁎ A Prospectus, with specimen page, may be had of the Publishers.

Longer Latin Exercises, Part I. Third Edition. 8vo. 4s.

The object of this Work is to supply boys with an easy collection of *short* passages, as an Exercise Book for those who have gone once, at least, through the First Part of the Editor's "Practical Introduction to Latin Prose Composition."

Longer Latin Exercises, Part II.; containing a Selection of Passages of greater length, in genuine idiomatic English, for Translation into Latin. 8vo. 4s.

Materials for Translation into Latin: selected and arranged by Augustus Grotefend. Translated from the German by the Rev. H. H. Arnold, B.A., with Notes and Excursuses. Third Edition. 8vo. 7s. 6d.

A Copious and Critical English-Latin Lexicon, by the Rev. T. K. Arnold and the Rev. J. E. Riddle. Sixth Edition. 1l. 5s.

An Abridgment of the above Work, for the Use of Schools. By the Rev. J. C. Ebden, late Fellow and Tutor of Trinity Hall, Cambridge. Square 12mo. *bound*. 10s. 6d.

The First Greek Book; on the Plan of "Henry's First Latin Book." Fourth Edition. 12mo. 5s.

The Second Greek Book (on the same Plan); containing an Elementary Treatise on the Greek Particles and the Formation of Greek Derivatives. 12mo. 5s. 6d.

A Practical Introduction to Greek Accidence. With Easy Exercises and Vocabulary. Seventh Edition. 8vo. 5s. 6d.

A Practical Introduction to Greek Prose Composition, Part I.
Ninth Edition. 8vo. 5s. 6d.

The object of this Work is to enable the Student, as soon as he can decline and conjugate with tolerable facility, to translate simple sentences after given examples, and with given words; the principles trusted to being principally those of *imitation and very frequent repetition*. It is at once a Syntax, a Vocabulary, and an Exercise Book.

Professor Madvig's Syntax of the Greek Language, especially of the Attic Dialect; translated by the Rev. Henry Browne, M.A. Together with an Appendix on the Greek Particles; by the Translator. Square 8vo. 8s. 6d.

An Elementary Greek Grammar. 12mo. 5s.; or, with Dialects, 6s.

A Complete Greek and English Lexicon for the Poems of Homer, and the Homeridæ. Translated from the German of Crusius, by Professor Smith. New and Revised Edition. 9s. *half-bound*.

*** A Prospectus and specimen of this Lexicon may be had.

A Copious Phraseological English-Greek Lexicon, founded on a work prepared by J. W. Frädersdorff, Ph. Dr. of the Taylor-Institution, Oxford. Revised, Enlarged, and Improved by the Rev. T. K. Arnold, M.A., formerly Fellow of Trinity College, Cambridge, and Henry Browne, M.A., Vicar of Pevensey, and Prebendary of Chichester. Third Edition, corrected, with the Appendix incorporated. 8vo. 21s.

*** A Prospectus, with specimen page, may be had.

Classical Examination Papers. A Series of 93 Extracts from Greek, Roman, and English Classics for Translation, with occasional Questions and Notes; each extract on a separate leaf. Price of the whole in a specimen packet, 4s., or six copies of any Separate Paper may be had for 3d.

Keys to the following may be had by Tutors only:

First Latin Book, 1s.   Second Latin Book, 2s.
Cornelius Nepos, 1s.
First Verse Book, 1s.   Latin Verse Composition, 2s.
Latin Prose Composition, Parts I. and II., 1s. 6d. each.
Longer Latin Exercises, Part I., 1s. 6d.   Part II., 2s. 6d.
Greek Prose Composition, Part I., 1s. 6d.   Part II., 4s. 6d.
First Greek Book, 1s. 6d.   Second, 2s.

MESSRS. RIVINGTON'S CATALOGUE. 21

The First Hebrew Book; on the Plan of "Henry's First Latin Book." 12mo. Second Edition. 7s. 6d.   The Key, 3s. 6d.

The Second Hebrew Book, containing the Book of Genesis; together with a Hebrew Syntax, and a Vocabulary and Grammatical Commentary. 9s.

The First German Book; on the Plan of "Henry's First Latin Book." By the Rev. T. K. Arnold and Dr. Frädersdorff. Fifth Edition. 12mo. 5s. 6d.   The Key, 2s. 6d.

A Reading Companion to the First German Book; containing Extracts from the best Authors, with a Vocabulary and Notes. 12mo. Second Edition. 4s.

The First French Book; on the Plan of "Henry's First Latin Book." Fifth Edition. 12mo. 5s. 6d.   Key to the Exercises, by Delille, 2s. 6d.

Henry's English Grammar; a Manual for Beginners. 12mo. 3s. 6d.

Spelling turned Etymology. Second Edition. 12mo. 2s. 6d.

The Pupil's Book, (a Companion to the above,) 1s. 3d.

Latin viâ English; being the Second Part of the above Work. 12mo. 4s. 6d.

An English Grammar for Classical Schools; being a Practical Introduction to "English Prose Composition." Sixth Edition. 12mo. 4s. 6d.

Arnold's Handbooks for the Classical Student, with Questions.

Ancient History and Geography. Translated from the German of Pütz, by the Ven. Archdeacon Paul. Second Edition. 12mo. 6s. 6d.

Mediæval History and Geography. Translated from the German of Pütz. By the same. 12mo. 4s. 6d.

Modern History and Geography. Translated from the German of Pütz. By the same. 12mo. 5s. 6d.

Grecian Antiquities. By Professor Bojesen. Translated from the German Version of Dr. Hoffa. By the same. Second Edition. 12mo. 3s. 6d.

Roman Antiquities. By Professor Bojesen. Second Edition. 3s. 6d.

Hebrew Antiquities. By the Rev. Henry Browne, M.A. Prebendary of Chichester. 12mo. 4s.

⁎ This Work describes the manners and customs of the ancient Hebrews which were common to them with other nations, and the rites and ordinances which distinguished them as the chosen people Israel.

Greek Synonymes. From the French of Pillon. 6s. 6d.

Latin Synonymes. From the German of Döderlein. Translated by the Rev. H. H. Arnold. Second Edition. 4s.

Arnold's School Classics.

Cornelius Nepos, Part I.; with Critical Questions and Answers, and an imitative Exercise on each Chapter. Fourth Edition. 12mo. 4s.

Eclogæ Ovidianæ, with English Notes; Part I. (from the Elegiac Poems.) Tenth Edition. 12mo. 2s. 6d.

Eclogæ Ovidianæ, Part II. (from the Metamorphoses.) 5s.

The Æneid of Virgil, with English Notes from Dübner. 12mo. 6s.

The Works of Horace, followed by English Introductions and Notes, abridged and adapted for School use, from the Edition of Fr. Dübner. In one volume, 12mo. 7s.

Cicero.—Selections from his Orations, with English Notes, from the best and most recent sources. Contents:—The Fourth Book of the Impeachment of Verres, the Four Speeches against Catiline, and the Speech for the Poet Archias. 12mo. Second Edition. 4s.

Cicero, Part II.; containing Selections from his Epistles, arranged in the order of time, with Accounts of the Consuls, Events of each year, &c. With English Notes from the best Commentators, especially Matthiæ. 12mo. 5s.

Cicero, Part III.; containing the Tusculan Disputations (entire). With English Notes from Tischer, by the Rev. Archdeacon Paul. Second Edition. 5s. 6d.

Cicero, Part IV.; containing De Finibus Malorum et Bonorum. (On the Supreme Good.) With a Preface, English Notes, &c., partly from Madvig and others, by the Rev. James Beaven, D.D., late Professor of Theology in King's College, Toronto. 12mo. 5s. 6d.

Cicero, Part V.; containing Cato Major, sive De Senectute Dialogus; with English Notes from Sommerbrodt, by the Rev. Henry Browne, M.A., Canon of Chichester. 12mo. 2s. 6d.

Homer for Beginners.—The First Three Books of the Iliad, with English Notes; forming a sufficient Commentary for Young Students. Second Edition. 12mo. 3s. 6d.

Homer.—The Iliad Complete, with English Notes and Grammatical References. Second Edition. In one thick volume, 12mo. *half-bound*. 12s.

In this Edition, the Argument of each Book is divided into short Sections, which are prefixed to those portions of the Text, respectively, which they describe. The Notes (principally from Dübner) are at the foot of each page. At the end of the volume are useful Appendices.

Homer.—The Iliad, Books I. to IV.; with a Critical Introduction, and copious English Notes. Second Edition. 12mo. 7s. 6d.

Demosthenes, with English Notes from the best and most recent sources, Sauppe, Doberenz, Jacobs, Dissen, Westermann, &c.

>The Olynthiac Orations. Second Edition. 12mo. 3s.
>The Oration on the Crown. Second Edition. 12mo. 4s. 6d.
>The Philippic Orations. Second Edition. 12mo. 4s.

Æschines.—Speech against Ctesiphon. 12mo. 4s.

The Text is that of *Baiter* and *Sauppe;* the Notes are by Professor Champlin, with additional Notes by President Woolsey and the Editor.

Sophocles, with English Notes, from Schneidewin. By the Rev. Archdeacon Paul, and the Rev. Henry Bowne, M.A.

>The Ajax. 3s.—The Philoctetes. 3s—The Œdipus Tyrannus. 4s.—The Œdipus Coloneus. 4s.—The Antigone. 4s.

Euripides, with English Notes, from Hartung, Dübner, Witzschel, Schöne, &c.

>The Hecuba.—The Hippolytus.—The Bacchæ.—The Medea.—The Iphigenia in Tauris, 3s. *each*.

Aristophanes.—Eclogæ Aristophanicæ, with English Notes, by Professor Felton. Part I. (The Clouds.) 12mo. 3s. 6d. Part II. (The Birds.) 3s. 6d.

⁎ *In this Edition the objectionable passages are omitted.*

THE
FOLLOWING CATALOGUES AND LISTS

MAY BE HAD GRATIS OF

MESSRS. RIVINGTON.

An Alphabetical List of all their Publications, in abridged titles, with the number of the Edition, the date of publication, and the price.

A Complete Classified Catalogue of Messrs. Rivington's School-books, with the Titles in full.

A separate List of the Rev. T. K. Arnold's School-books. (These are included in the complete School Catalogue.)

A Prospectus of Three Lexicons, with specimen pages.

A List of New Publications, issued quarterly.

A List of Works suitable for Book-hawking Societies and Parochial Libraries.

A Catalogue of Bibles and Prayer Books, printed by the Cambridge University Press.

A List of Theological, Classical, and other Works, edited for the Syndics of the Cambridge Press.

A List of the Publications of the Anglo-Continental Society.

RIVINGTONS, LONDON AND OXFORD.

www.ingramcontent.com/pod-product-compliance
Lightning Source LLC
Chambersburg PA
CBHW020254170426
43202CB00008B/370